BRONX

BIANNUAL No. 2

**edited by
Miles Marshall Lewis**

All names, characters, places, and incidents in the fiction chapters of this collection are the product of the authors' imaginations. Any resemblance to real events or persons, living or dead, is entirely coincidental.

Published by Akashic Books
©2007 *Bronx Biannual*/Miles Marshall Lewis

ISBN-13: 978-1-933354-09-5
ISBN-10: 1-933354-09-7
Library of Congress ISSN Control Number: 1932-6394

First printing

Bronx Biannual
c/o Akashic Books
PO Box 1456
New York, NY 10009
info@akashicbooks.com
www.akashicbooks.com

Contents

Introduction

This is the origin story of BRONX BIANNUAL.

Early on the morning of my birthday three years ago, my partner and I woke up talking—mainly about her older brother's marriage. I tried to fall back asleep but couldn't, and eventually, at eight o'clock, our alarm went off. For my birthday, she'd planned a surprise weekend in Deauville, a small town over two hours away on the Atlantic coast of France, known for its annual American film festival. We got dressed, packed, and headed out in her dad's Renault.

But as I had lain in bed, unsuccessfully trying to return to sleep, I'd thought about the direction of my life's work (par for the course on a birthday morning). Many artists do their greatest, most defining work in their thirties. In 2004, at thirty-three, I felt I'd just crossed a major line by publishing my first book. The release party, the reviews, the interviews, the tour . . . all led up to a sinking feeling of *Now what?* I thought, lying there in bed, that two artists' work in particular had elements I wanted to integrate into my own oeuvre by the time I'm forty: Dave Eggers and Andy Warhol.

Eggers was an editor and writer at Salon.com. He launched a zine in the nineties called *Might*. He published a memoir at twenty-nine and got raves. It firmly established his twentysomething white-guy style (raised on MTV and *Seinfeld*) of using irony, humor, and postmodernism, rooting it all in a firm knowledge of literature. He and David Foster Wallace rule this, but Eggers built a cottage industry. *McSweeney's* came from the ashes of *Might*: a literary journal that young white guys would actually read, full of writers who sort of mirror Eggers's aesthetic. Then there was McSweeneys.net, full of writing that couldn't make the journal—also a holding place for all things Eggers, essentially a DaveEggers.com. He started 826 Valencia, a not-for-profit to teach high schoolers how to write, out in Cali. (There are several branches now, including one in Brooklyn.) He opened a store like Spike Lee's old Spike's Joint called McSweeney's in Park Slope. He started editing an annual Best American Series book, *Best American Nonrequired Reading,* sort of a *McSweeney's* full of material published places other than *McSweeney's*. Then he launched *The Believer*, a monthly literary magazine. (I eventually contributed to *The Believer*; my interview with the late playwright August Wilson was reprinted in *The Believer Book of Writers Talking to Writers*.) No ads, no photos, eight dollars a pop. And put out by McSweeney's Books, which has brought out Neal Pollack and others. Like George Lucas financing his own films, Eggers publishes his own books through McSweeney's. He doesn't even need book deals with major houses, he can credibly publish his books through his own recognized independent, mass scale. (He does choose major houses for the paperback editions of some of his books.)

I toyed with the idea of starting a magazine for years. I interned on the launch issue of *Vibe* and witnessed other nascent hiphop mags get their start during the nineties: *XXL*, *Honey*. Reading about the origins of the *New Yorker* and *Rolling Stone* would always get me excited and inspired about making my own. I've seen *Wax Poetics*, a journal concerned with the hiphop aesthetic, do some cool-looking stuff. I didn't want to do the "urban" version of *The Believer*, or anything really like that. Hiphop critic Marcus Reeves put out two issues of *TellSpin*, an independent hiphop literary mag, but it was financed from the dotcom boom, so they went bust around 2000.

That fateful birthday morning, I envisioned a magazine or journal called *Bronx*, to make of it whatever I wanted to. I liked the idea of giving back to the youth as well, maybe harnessing the best and brightest creative minds of black colleges for some joint project. Could English majors at Morehouse, Spelman, Howard, Hampton, etc. form the staff of *Bronx*, a hiphop-styled *New Yorker/McSweeney's?*

Andy Warhol was first and foremost a painter, an artist. Whatever else he did was rooted in his success as an artist. But he threw happenings in the sixties like the Exploding Plastic Inevitable, parties that combined film, music, and art. The Velvet Underground would perform before they were even signed; movies were projected against the walls through lava lamp–like lenses, and artwork adorned walls. Warhol ended up "producing" the debut VU record, hooking them up with Nico and providing subject matter for songs like "All Tomorrow's Parties." As an artist, he did cover artwork for that album, and for the Rolling Stones' *Sticky Fingers*.

Around this time, he branched out into underground independent film, many starring Joe Dallesandro (the guy in the underwear modeling for *Sticky Fingers*), and they were panned—but they exist: *Flesh*, *Heat*, *Trash*, and many more. Plus, he started *Interview* magazine and published *The Philosophy of Andy Warhol*. Many of those happenings took place at his Batcave-like workspace/office/headquarters The Factory. He was a svengali, creating protégé "superstars" from the fringes of East Village society—a lot of transsexuals, gays, and S/M types.

I attended Brooklyn parties like the Crash House and the Brooklyn Tea Party in my twenties with some of the same flavor: people smoking herb, performing, movies playing silently on VCRs, artwork hanging on the walls. And Brooklyn was just the scene for that, especially in the mid-nineties days of spoken word. I thought it would be great to find a loft space, set up all the necessary ingredients for a hiphop happening centered around *Bronx* magazine, book a local band like Tamar-Kali or Mrk Drkfthr, and see what happens.

I ultimately decided to found the journal you hold in your hands, talking it all out on the drive from Paris to Deauville. A twice-a-year literary magazine called BRONX BIANNUAL; a skeleton staff of juniors from various black colleges—internships for them. A grand premiere issue featuring fiction, essays, and poetry. I'd take inspiration from *The Crisis*, *Fire!!*, and any other old black lit mags I could get my hands on.

The intention with BRONX BIANNUAL is to publish both celebrated and unsung writers on a variety of subjects germane to the black aesthetic. Urbane urban literature: bourgeois yet boulevard. BRONX BIANNUAL is fluid like water. No guiding manifesto per se, no set format, with a concept in mind of what The Factory might've come up with had Warhol put out a literary journal. Like *XXL* edited by Rhodes Scholars at Oxford, or *Vanity Fair* edited at The Point in the South Bronx.

This edition's round-robin passing of the literary microphone between fifteen different scribes is a mixtape in print. (Did I just master-mix metaphors?) The protagonist of writer Bahiyyih Davis's "The Story of My Hair" struggles with her share of bad hair days, as well as the eternal oreo conflict between her competing love for both Lollapalooza and Mary J.

Blige. "Church of the Living Womb Manifesto for Haters" is poet Liza Jessie Peterson's sweet kiss-off to untold would-be usurpers of Zora Neale Hurston's legacy that will leave you wondering if it's live or if it's Memorex. "The Wu-Tang Candidate" is my own tale of rapper Ace Boon Coon's modern-day minstrel show; read between the lines. We believe in sometimes going long (Davis's story is a *New Yorker*-ish 14,000-plus words) but short-and-sweet stories work their own wonders—"The Egg Man" is Sun Singleton's succinct meditation on forgiveness through gastronomy. World Fantasy Award–winner Sheree Renée Thomas takes us through hell via "Malaika Descending." Michael A. Gonzales makes his second BRONX BIANNUAL appearance, another stab at the hiphop Chester Himes crown, with his Harlem jazz-age story, "Blues for Sister Rose."

"Born Again" brings us back to the modern age: poet t'ai freedom ford's spin on urban teenage love. D. Scot Miller draws us into the proverbial rabbit hole of a graffiti mural with "Knot Frum Hear." Novelist Kenji Jasper gives a taste of his work-in-progress, an excerpt entitled "Friday." Breaking up the stretch of fiction is SékouWrites's poetic account of racism, "Love, Rage, and Volkswagens." Jerry A. Rodriguez contributes the issue's near-obligatory superhero story (we love long johns and capes around here), "Marine Tiger." Esteemed poet Staceyann Chin confronts the Hurricane Katrina aftermath of New Orleans with "Walk amidst the Broken Beds." No sooner does Bronx native kelly a. abel relate her harrowing street narrative of a young girl's sexual abuse in "Broke-Down Princess" than a pimp gets his comeuppance for nearly the same crime in Carol Taylor's Iceberg Slim–inspired short, "A Debt to Pay." The muted remembrance of Natasha Labaze's heartfelt "Love Letter to Haiti" closes the issue.

There it is.

Miles Marshall Lewis
Paris, France
May 2007

The Story of My Hair

by Bahiyyih Davis

W hen the Irish love the Irish they make themselves a human hair ring for the wrist. A woman wears it on her wedding day, and the ring is symbolic of a love that loops forever and ever. The hair is just a nasty twist.

In my parents' wedding pictures the colors are dull. It is a park, a rainy day. My mother's dress is dingy and loose like a slip; he wears linen that exposes his bare brown chest and has brushed his 'fro into the shape of a heart. There is a circle of witnesses, none of them my white or black grand-parents. People have brought hot dishes in foil to pass. My mother has baked the cake from a box. A random guest has been asked to photograph.

In one picture a color pokes through. It is the red of Mom's short curly hair. Later it will darken and stop kidding itself. Released, it will sleep straight and brown on her shoulders for the rest of her life. But right now it is deep red like half of my roots. Our clan of pale, freckled Nesbits, unaware that someone on the Scotch-Irish border might have sent her a hairy bracelet if they had known.

They go honeymooning in a tent anchored to the forest floor of the Wisconsin wild. For years their genes practice mixing, until finally out comes my brother, who looks nothing like either one. Has Dizzy Gillespie cheeks and hair that glides effortlessly through a small-toothed comb, almost straight when chopped short. He has a straight nose and a forest of eyebrows.

Then I come, two steps behind, a pee-colored version of my father. His wide nose and eyes that slant, eyes that will cause even Asians to ask if I'm one of them. I'm his little light clone. Except for the hair, which from the beginning is thick and big and almost impenetrable, even with a variety of tools. My black grandmother and temporary lineup of aunts-in-law call it nappy and my mother has to laugh it off. No, it isn't, she insists, just curly!—but they laugh at her, shaking their heads, and beg to differ. I learn to crawl, walk, and speak peeking out from under a mound of coils. Hair that won't be silenced or softened. A net. A trap. A force field.

A majority of first memories start in pictures and spread across the mind: me on a lap, on a blanket, chewing on a teether against the black background of nighttime in the picture window of our first house. My brother as He-Man, The Most Powerful Man in the Universe, my father on all fours as Battle Cat, and me as She-Ra, the Princess of Power, with a Happy Meal box balanced on top of my ponytail as a colorful crown. There is me and a black puppy. Me in a pink tutu, me in a blue leotard, a silver bucket over my head.

But without the influence of snapshots my real life begins with not wanting to lose my hair. In a grocery store I'm four, tiny enough to still fit in the front of a screeching metal cart. My mother, comparing prices on healthy cereal, has her back turned to me but her fingers keep touch through my knee.

A witch comes up. She's leaning against her cart and shaking all over like she's scared or cold. She has long teeth and brown spots on her skin and sore patches of missing hair.

She's stopped right next to me, whispering, "Can I have a curl? Just one?" And she's reaching out to take it with a hooked finger. I scream at the top of my lungs and almost fall to the floor reaching for safety. The witch takes her hand back slowly and my mother and her are both giggling. They say something back and forth and more laughing but it is all muffled to me; I have my head hidden in my mother's braless breasts.

When I look up the witch is gone. My mother, brushing my cheeks with the backs of her cold hands, moves us to another aisle, to the toppings and spices. "It's okay," she's repeating. "She wasn't really going to take your hair."

When kindergarten starts my hair is long enough to be able to hide in single thick braids, or Pippi Longstocking pigtail ones, in cinnamon roll–size buns, under hats and headbands. The older I get the more I hate it but cutting it off would only be worse. I don't know and can't even imagine a girl with hair any shorter than her shoulders.

There are nightly battles in the bath over the importance of combing. This has been going on for years. She interrupts my perfectly good time by entering the small bright bathroom with a sigh and a bottle of tangle-negotiating conditioner. I always agree to be good. But somewhere around the middle I lose it. I scream at every pull and spin so she can't reach the back, what I call the *underneath*, what one side of my family calls your *kitchen* and the other side has no right to nickname.

"You have to comb your hair!" she says, half a notch under a yell.

"No! You don't know how to do it right!" I have been preaching to her for nearly a decade about how to hold it tight right at the root, how to start at the tips and work her way slowly and patiently inward. But since she won't listen I now scream, "Let *me*!"

But she doesn't. Instead she goes through a sequence of pleading, leaving the room to breathe, coming back with small threats disguised as decisions.

"Fine," she sighs. "We'll just cut it off."

When the knots are finally conquered it is hours past bedtime, my body pruned, the water gray and cold.

Night after night we fight. Until at age ten I finally win. It comes unexpectedly. My mother gives up in the middle of thrashing her way through the black jungle, throws up her hands, and storms out. She's left the black comb suspended in a gnarled chunk. I work it out and stare at it in my hands.

So now we don't talk about my hair. The conversation is over. I walk by her in the morning with an independent air. She probably notices the knot forming on the top right side but bites her lips to teach me a long-deserved lesson. Or maybe she is relieved to be through with it and doesn't even look—is sick of looking at it, maybe it gives her nightmares. Plus it is usually hidden inside a frizzy bun and under a black and bright-pink puff paint New Kids on the Block baseball hat that doesn't match anything.

I have been screaming for days, in both bathrooms and at night in the tub and in front of the body-length mirror that's screwed to the hallway under the dim chandelier. My crying is tainting the air of the house but people do not demand or even request that I shut up. They walk around me with unstable stacks of dinner dishes and paper grocery bags and laundry to be taken upstairs, and they are respectfully silent, trying to avoid being smacked by a frantic flying hand or a blind insult or a whirling plastic comb.

My hair has joined itself at the top, hardened, tumorized. It's a black fuzzy goiter, grayed in spots by the white baby powder Sarah sprinkled trying to make me look elderly. It was a game we had going. I wore her stepdad's old trench coat and spoke in the octave of a frog. It was funny but now the laughter has trickled to a stop. I pick and pull it but there's no progress. I beg, I butter it up with squirt after pointless squirt of No More Tangles. Ever since I fired my mother from combing it hasn't gotten much quality attention. I haven't been going all the way through or underneath because it brings on pain beyond my threshold. I surface-brush and hide it all in my stretched purple scrunchie. Now it will have to be thrown away and grown again slowly from scratch.

I yank on it one final time and pray for a breakthrough, squeezing my eyes as I attempt to tear. When I release I know it just hangs like a water balloon, flopping against my right ear when I stand to walk. My mother, waiting patiently behind this round door, is holding a Diet Coke, her green bottomless purse, and keys.

"I'm sorry," she says, her hand on my shoulder out the back door.

The shop isn't far, just outside of walkable. I wipe tears in the light reflection of myself that shows in the passenger window of this rattling Trooper. I refuse to take the dose of music she offers. I concentrate on clearing my face of tear evidence, even though it won't matter. It is no longer a face with recognizable features, but a hot blotchy hive, the eye area raised pink.

We pull up and stall, listening to the engine. I flick the knot with a finger. It barely moves. Finally my mother takes a breath, unclips her seat belt and mine, and turns the key, yanks it out, pops the handle, and the door is ajar. There are no more sounds left to make unless I'm going to scream again.

We get out and cross the street. There is no traffic and no outlet at the end. The salon looks dark and closed but it's only an illusion. The knot on top of my head is a yarmulke.

I don't have a regular place because I hardly ever get my hair touched or tampered with. Never more than a semi-annual trim. My mother has picked a black salon because she thinks they will know what to do with me and my texture. I can't imagine how anyone will manage to make it look anything but bald and hysterical.

When we come in they are laughing loud and crisp, washing heads in the way, way back. There are two customers and many stylists. Everyone takes a pause to look at us chiming our way through the blue door.

"I have an appointment for this," my mother tells them. She's touching the knot with a flat palm until I squirm away.

Two women approach, quick-stepping like it's an emergency, and before I can step back they have their long, stiff nails stabbed into the mess I've made. One lets her mouth drop and a gasp escape. The other is shaking her head at me but smiling. "Sweetie, what happened?" My mom has brought a novel to read.

I am sat backwards at the sink. They don't talk to me much but when they do it is soft and smooth. "Lean back, baby," "You tell me, now, if the water too hot," "Look at all this curly hair," and, "Don't worry, girl. It'll come back." They are all big-chested and flower-smelling, flashing thin gold necklaces when they lean over me for the shampoo. They make me feel dumb for all my screaming and blaming. And I want aunts instead of all the divorced uncles I have.

Water drips on my shoulders, rolling down the protective plastic over my lap. This shop is dark and plays the classic R&B station. I catch a shot of my mother peeking over her paperback at me. I hear the big lady behind the counter break her humming every once in a while to speak to her and she just laughs back.

The small woman behind me in the mirror is chewing spearmint gum and imagining all outcomes. She's running over it gently and tilting her head at every possibility and it feels like it might not be so bad when it's through. "I'm gonna make you look pretty," she decides. "So yo' Chinese Daddy will be proud."

I want to tell her no, not Chinese, *black*, like them. There is a reason we came here, I want her to know. But I nod and close my eyes when she spins me away from myself.

The knot falls to the floor with a dull thud. The hair that wasn't tangled falls after it, must be sacrificed, covers the knot, and it is all swept in a pile like curled dead leaves. Tears are forming but it will be okay. Even though she keeps clipping. And the scissors swipe my ear. And I can feel it going way too far. And there's sawdust lumping in the top of my throat. I don't want it this short but I can't even squeak. She's going to form it into something. Not just leave remains. She's singing along to the radio as she snips so it must be—

"O-kaaay."

She turns me quickly and I'm not ready so my vision spins, I wobble side-to-side in the high chair. My hair is all gone and boyishly awkward. There is no style, no purpose to the cut. It's worse than just a boy, it's like a sloppy boy, like my brother when he can't get an appointment at the barber. My head is adorned in a crown of dark, dry grass. My cheeks have fattened and it's not from the crying. I look like I'm storing fat for the winter. My face has given up five years to this haircut. No boy will ever want to be dared to kiss me. I look like a tall baby, a small lesbian.

She helps me up by the elbow and brushes my shoulders with a tiny silk broom. My mom pays and I stand at her side in a daze.

"You like it?" they ask.

"Yep. I like it."

"Bet you'll comb it!"

The shop is so big right now. All the other customers have gone and it's closing time. Someone is sweeping against the clock and the music has stopped.

"Thank you!" my mother calls back inside as we leave.

Before the car doors close around me I am bawling, trying to pull on my hair but my fingers slip. My mother is rubbing my back but I don't want her to. It will take years to grow to any kind of length and in the meantime I won't go anywhere, especially school.

"Let's go home," she's saying. I'm crumbled into my lap. "Bet it will look better once we wash it." She thinks water will bring my curls back but I know how really gone they are.

She starts the car and I feel it in my stomach. We're rolling away. I want to be older than this haircut but I can't stop crying. My tear ducts are struggling to keep up with how I feel. She plays scales on my back with her fingers as she drives, comfort taps. And it's more of a whimper now.

The cut never looks better. Not when washed or gelled or given a few days' perspective. It's horrible, and there is nothing to do but pray that it grows faster than the dark part of my genes wants to allow.

On my first Monday as a boy I wear one of my new weapons, a white-and-purple-striped shirt with a hood attached, a hood that is thin and stretchy and was probably never meant to actually be worn. I pull the drawstrings so that everything above the eyes and just below the bottom lip is sealed from public view. No one asks me to remove it or even what's wrong. Because they've all seen the knot—they know. I don't plan on letting people see it, not in their whole lives. I have several more hoodies at home, and scarves my mom insists make me look like a cancer patient. I am busy brainstorming new disguises almost all the time.

At lunch I am seated at my desk group, silently chewing a sandwich, concentrating hard on keeping my head positioned just right so that the hood stays put. So hard that I don't even see or sense the approach of Marcus, a boy a year older than me, skinny and blue-eyed, a crew cut and glasses, a pug nose that is constantly raw under the nostrils, who my brother and the rest of the seventh grade have renamed Carcass, an insult he doesn't appreciate and enjoys taking out on me.

Carcass yanks at the back of my hood so fast that by the time my hands react and fly up to resist the pull, it is already down, fallen like a parachute around my shoulders, and my head with its embarrassment of a haircut is on display.

"Carc!" I yell, so loud that the majority of the class who hasn't yet looked over now does. Even the teachers are watching and have that sad, head-cocked-in-pity look covering up their urges to giggle. The rest of the class isn't so restrained. Laughter is bouncing from desk to desk like a beachball. Then quickly dying down and merging back into secret-telling and chewing, but I am nested into my arms on the cold tabletop and won't come out. Not even when Carc is sent up behind my hunched back to cough out a stale apology. I reach back to hit him and he laughs again, runs away to cause trouble elsewhere. Nobody likes him. A teacher is at my side now, crouched down.

"It's really not bad," she whispers, with breath that smells like ham. "You had to take it off sometime anyway, right?"

She excuses me to the bathroom and I run out. I spend the rest of lunch in the long mirrors trying to come to grips with it, how I look, how I will look for a long, long time. I've never thought I was breathtaking, but I have wanted to be, dreamed of beauty, hoped maybe that I was at least growing into it. But now I am seeing ugliness at its truest and rawest, uncovered and throbbing without a shield of hair. And realizing that I will always see it. Even if the curls grow back thicker and more spiral, spinning down past my ankles. I know what I really look like underneath and it isn't pretty.

When a girl comes to get me I follow her back with my head down but exposed, sit behind everyone for a chapter of *Jurassic Park* on the rug. I am waiting for it, but no one turns around to snicker, not today or for the rest of the haircut. No one points and clutches their abdominal muscles when I come down the hall or attaches the first letter of my name to something like Bob or Brandon. Nobody rubs at it roughly like a dog or draws cruel doodles or even mentions it. But my cheeks stay red in anticipation for months.

Our school is all-white, progressive, and private, an education that we can't really afford. But we have to go here so that we will grow up to be artists instead of doctors or lawyers or juvenile delinquents who disappoint our parents. Our mother has invented a position in the small staff so that they waive our tuition year after year. She is the drama teacher, even though it's our father who is the actor, who gave up professional acting when I was five to finally feed us. She was a stay-at-home mom and mime, who now suddenly has to talk hundreds of children through her silent, suspended moves.

To balance the color in our lives we have moved across town to the West Side, into an enormous red-brick house that's underpriced to make up for its modest surroundings. On our drive from one side of the bridge to the other my brother stared hard out the window.

"Are we in Chicago?" he asked.

"Why?"

"Because," he whispered, "there's black people."

The black half of our family all live in Chicago, a city we only surface-scrape on Thanksgivings and occasional summer Sundays when our father feels guilty for keeping us a safe two hours away. Visits are always dished out in hours, usually four but sometimes as many as six or as little as two, and tainted with foods I don't eat—boiled cabbage that smells musty in the pot, black-eyed peas that are supposed to bring good luck for the new year—and also a discomfort that emits from my uncle, who greets me at the front door calling me beautiful, not as an adjective, but as a name starting with a capital, as in, "Hey, Beautiful, lemme get your coat," and I like it better when he decides to call me Big Face instead, but even this is said with a wink and a smile. And then the vibe from my two girl cousins, who share this uncle as a father and also a cushion on the couch. One is almost as light as me but without the curls or the shyness; there is no mistaking her for anything less than black. The other is older and darker than both of us, softer and more proper-spoken than her sister, and also an avid collector of purses.

Besides the couch and one parent they also share a strong Chicago accent and a deep love for Barbie and her sexy entourage. So whenever we go I drag mine out of the closet and brush them off at my mother's request.

This is how it goes every holiday: I walk in humbly. The cousins are elbowed into waving at me from where they sit slouched toward the TV and then verbally coaxed by our grandma to lead me down the stairs in the back of the kitchen with armloads of dolls and accessories in spectrums of pink. I have two, both given to me at birthday parties by guests my mother invited. One is blonde and inherently bitchy, the second came with a lei that's been lost but she still knows how to hula. Another was black and bought for me on a bonding trip to a drugstore where our grandmother spent thirty of her Social Security dollars on identical dolls for the three of us, so we'd all have something the same, but mine, somewhere between here and home, was lost or stolen or ignored into a sudden and untragic disappearance.

My cousins, of course, still have and cherish theirs. They have a total of about twenty of the same small woman, brownie-black with smooth, straight features, and no variations in hairstyles except the ones my cousins have imposed. Like a short blunt cut that ends unevenly along a fragile jaw line, or one with a head of microscopic braids that took hours and you better not touch, just like the real heads of the cousins who hold them.

My cousins haven't seen my new haircut yet but they've heard. By the time I am pulled along to see them it's had a good month of solid growing. Still, for the first time it is shorter than both of theirs. It is being restrained from sticking straight up in the front by the brute force of a thick purple headband. Now, against the plea of the gel and spray, it arcs up at the middle like the McDonald's sign—something people can catch a glimpse of and recognize from miles away. My uncle still gives me his greeting, but this time it comes out slow and strained, as if it's an effort for him to make me feel like the special girl I once was. And for the first time, my cousins are smiling. They wave before my grandmother's nudge reaches them and they scoop up the Barbies before I break out of my coat.

"Hey, Dawn," they say together, because it's my middle name and they call me that. "Come on, Dawn." They drag me away. I am just waiting for one of them to release a string of disses based on what I look like from the eyebrows up.

We play in the concrete basement where our uncle in his soft brown cowboy hat sneaks away with his plate to eat alone. We stay in the corner on a square of red carpet. Sometimes Barbies get hurt and have to operate on each other with nothing but the miracle of their small sharp hands. But mostly they just change dresses and restyle their hair again and again. We brush and braid and twist and take out because it isn't what Barbie wants. We work her white miniskirt over the bubbling plastic hips and replace it with a black silky number, reconfigure her hair, mess it up, try again, get called upstairs for dessert and eat it quietly, then quickly go back to our dolls. We speak and joke and argue with each other through their rosy smiling mouths.

"You stuck up," my cousin's Barbie accuses my Hawaiian one.

"Well, you're just stupid then. And ugly," mine says back under her breath. If she weren't so plastic her yellow cheeks would redden, maybe she would run away if I wasn't holding her firmly in place by the grooves of her waist. My cousin's Barbie throws off her suit coat and approaches, flicks my Barbie's pink grass skirt, and stares her down until she feels like peeing.

"C'mon, y'all, time to go shopping." Another Barbie interrupts the catfight by driving right through it with her pink Ferrari and her delicate hand in the air.

We make them jump stiffly over the backseat and embrace. "Sorry, girl" and "That's okay!"

There is much giggling as they drive off swerving toward an imaginary mega-mall.

My favorite cousin Eraina and her older brother Brian are almost here, on their way for a one-week visit to our home for the first time in history. I am excited but nervous about what we will do, how we will possibly fill all these hot, empty hours with the kind of fun to rival with the city.

They arrive late and sleepy and we don't have to do anything but share our beds. Eraina snores. And talks through her dreams, tosses and turns. In the morning she wakes up later than the rest of the house and wanders downstairs with hair that is wide-awake and waving hello. She asks for cereal but is appalled that we drink skim instead of whole milk. I sit next to her, watching her face contort as she tries to swallow. "I didn't know you liked whole," my mother apologizes. "I'll get some." She runs to the store and the four of us sit watching cartoons in awkwardness.

When Eraina attempts to do her hair she discovers that there's no grease or picks under the sink of either bathroom and summons me, yelling my name up the stairs. "Where your grease at?" she asks as I arrive, winded, in the half-bath doorway. I stare and blink and turn red. "You don't use grease in your hair?" she says, smiling, slowly getting it. I shake my head. She giggles a little and steps past me asking for her Uncle George. My father runs to his closet to retrieve a small jar with a white lid. She takes it back to the bathroom and shuts the door. I am on the other side, still blushing, deeply confused.

It's my brother's idea for a water fight. We've exhausted almost all our other ideas, computer games and kidnap and jail and taking turns on bikes, with days and days left uneaten before us. Luckily it is scorching and they have brought their suits.

It's girls against boys. Our brothers are both older and faster but somehow we are soaking them. Maybe they are letting us. We've hardly been hit with a drop and are sneaking around the front of the house with full buckets.

I douse Brian as he rounds the corner. He is standing in the lawn raining from his shorts and pretending to be mad. We are jumping and giving each other five and feeling like family. But here comes my brother with the long green hose looped around his hand about to let it go. I see him coming and run but don't have time to warn her and the white rush of water blasts up her back and over her head and into her ponytail. She is trying to get out of the direct spray but he has her and is following, the water gushing and gushing over and down her until the hose won't stretch anymore and snaps him back.

For a moment there is no sound. Then her mouth opens and a traffic-stopping scream is released. She has tears in her eyes and they are dripping faster than the water beads that hang from the strands of her ruined hair. Her fists are balled and she's heaving, then running at my brother and swinging, yelling insults that are unintelligible because of the pitch of her voice.

Brian catches her and holds her back with his whole body. "He didn't know! He ain't know!" He is trying to get through to one of her ears but she is still thrashing.

My brother is against the house now, shutting off the water and look-ing back with mouth dropped. Brian picks her up and carries her, arms slicing, legs bicycling, inside. The door is closed and we can still hear the screaming. I shrug at him and he shrugs back, our hearts beating, brains working in double-time.

She's hysterical and we are stuck at a standstill on the lawn, burning our skin in the sun and still very, very confused.

It isn't long before my hair makes its comeback, bigger and badder than before. It's surpassed my shoulders again and strengthened. I struggle with it, lay down the law in the morning, then tie it up and away.

I'm in the eighth grade and a full-on teen now. I can't bypass mirrors like I used to. If I try, they wink at the corners of my eyes and call me back. I stare, not sure what I'm looking for. Maybe waiting for the image to change into something amazing like those 3-D pictures I can never get inside. It's frustrating, like those pictures—a mirror now requires great focus and a perspective that maybe I don't have. Other people see space-ships and life at the deepest parts of the ocean and parades of dancing cir-cus animals. They say, "Oh yeah!" and get excited. I spend great spans of time standing there, appearing to be sucked into them but not breaking past the surface, only seeing a jumble of meaningless dots, seeing a girl with too much face and dry tangles spilling out of their cage, seeing noth-ing to get all happy about.

Something drastic must be done with me. So I'm in the kitchen under towels and tinfoil. My mother is worrying birdlike over my hair, hover-ing around to lift and relift the shiny pieces. We do not want singe or breakage.

This bleach is serious, the sting of it filling our wide kitchen. It's Saturday. We are watching Lifetime and waiting for the blonde to really, really show. My scalp is beginning to burn but I bounce my knees through it. After, I will soak the pale strips in red and green dyes the consistency of mayo, one color per side of my head. And tonight I will wear my blue poly-ester shirt that buttons, and my ripped jeans shorts, my Rainbow Brite leg warmers, and duct-taped combat boots. I will blacken my lips with eyeliner and this will be punk. I will leave the dyed pieces dangling out of my ponytail into my face and attach baby barrettes to the ends. I'm crazy over a white boy who may notice me more if I buzz bright like Christmas.

My mother, nervous, keeps looking again and again for the change. "It's ready," she insists, but it's golden and I want it to be sunshine.

When it's done I stand in front of the long mirror smiling. I wish I could do more but she still has possession over most of me and I can't ruin myself completely until I'm eighteen or out of this house. The dye will wash out in six to eight weeks. The bleach will grow out, or get cut once it's made its point.

I get dressed in my room so fast that I get sweaty under the arms and on the rim of my scalp. We pick up my friend across town and drive back to the West Side toward the Get-a-way, a playground for teens.

"Your hair . . . You did it! I love it!" my friend says. She was the one to suggest it, even though her own is limp and blonde, just the way her parents mixed it. She wears the same clean, unripped pair of jeans and a white shirt and flat yellow Converses. The fact that my hair has surprised her makes me look at it from different angles in the mirror the whole way, doubting myself and what I've done and where I am going.

When we are there my mother passes me five dollars and says to be careful under her breath. Look for her at ten-thirty. I get out and away from her Volkswagen as discreetly as possible.

Punks from around the city are streaming in through the open gates, colorful and pierced through the face. Inside the playground there are swings and one slide, monkey bars and a low beam, equipment that sits desolate and silent except weekend nights when local bands play on the small wooden stage. It's called a battle but usually it's not as confrontational as that. It's tucked back in the woods where there are no real neighbors, only a housing project down the street where noise is constant and no one can complain. Saturday is our night. Kids from my neighborhood will flock here tomorrow for hip-hop, but this year I am thirteen and not yet one of them.

There are shooting stars in the navy-blue sky and a big blond man at the entrance. He holds a flashlight beam onto the smiling face of my I.D.

to make sure I have a teen in my age. He looks quickly from me to my picture to match them.

"I just dyed my hair," I whisper, and feel dumb. He studies it once more and waves us in.

The music starts up as we walk in under the bridge. The screech of an electric guitar, the smashing of cymbals. I jump. The singer has a bleached mohawk that's dark and buzzed on the sides. He looks like a skunk and his singing comes from the top of the throat instead of the belly. Anyone can do this, I think, but I want to like it and see some beauty in their chaos.

White boys are plentiful, but the only one I love is tall and thin and has dirty-blond hair that comes into his eyes. He tosses it away by jerking his head and grins slow and crooked, has minty teeth and a straight nose. Most of all he has these blue eyes like clean pool water. His name is Jason and he's fifteen and doesn't look my way by accident.

"Look up," my friend says, and there he is, hanging over the bridge behind us with a Super Soaker.

"You guys wanna get wet?" he asks.

We yell and run away giggling but not far. He isn't the type of boy to squirt us anyway. He winks and disappears and I sit down at a picnic table by the port-a-potties.

"He's so into you," my friend says, her voice sad, and her face drops. I shake no. I want her to make an argument for it but she shrugs. She likes a boy too and is eye-surfing the crowd to find him. I think he has glasses and purple hair but I'm not sure 'cause I don't pay attention. I just adore Jason and want him to come talk to me and pull me aside and when we get married I want to have a whole team of his skinny pale babies.

The crowd isn't into the music. There isn't even an audience. People wander around the maze to smoke and do flips off the blue plastic swings. My friend and I do slow circles around the fence that holds everything. I'm looking for him in all the places where he could be. If he has left I'll want to call for an early ride.

My friend is kicking the rocks. "You look cute tonight," she sighs, but I itch like I'm in a costume. If I ever go to Chicago like this the black side of my family will sigh and shake their heads at each other. Then fix me a plate.

I love the red and green pieces but I hate the rest of me. Like the lower half of my body that stands out. White girls are obese, or small, fragile and flat, never in between, they have bodies with no imagination. They are simple and easy to handle. But I haven't even had my period more than a year and already my hips are wide enough to shoot out a screaming ten-pounder. Besides that, my butt is round, fleshy, and unjeanable. And my nostrils spread too far. And my hair, despite its new colors, is still the texture of a big ball of brown hay and cannot be smoothed or suppressed. When I overhear some white kid talking about "that black guy," I realize he doesn't see me or doesn't know what I am, which is so much worse than the possibility that he just doesn't care, and my heart races like I'm trying to hide in a closet and there are footsteps right outside my door.

So my white boy will never ever like me. If he did he wouldn't know what to do. I'm used to the short, muscular black boys who are my neighbors, who pound on my back door twice daily, chase me on their bikes, and tell my mother that I'm sexy. Jason would be too shy to come near my house. He might try, but my neighborhood is too full of salsa music and corn vendors, rap music and flavor. He would run or stand frozen and pissing in the middle of Montague Street, until maybe a white cop spotted him and escorted him, shaken but safe, back over the river.

"I'm thinking of cutting it all off," I say.

We are making a pendulum on two empty swings. A louder band has started and people have gone up front to mosh, which scares me.

"Don't," she says.

"I might," I threaten.

I won't. The night is cold and thin now. We wrap our arms around each other like scarves and jackets. We walk like this once more around.

This is the last band night of the season. We get to the gate and I don't see him. My eyes sting and start to fill. My friend is staring at her boy as he leans on a pole that supports this playground and laughs in the face of a girl whose black hair is interrupted in the middle by a thin pink streak. His hair is blue, not purple, and he doesn't wear glasses, or maybe he is somebody else.

"She's ugly," I offer, but so is this friend.

"Let's just go," she says.

There is a pay phone outside the gate. If we exit we cannot reënter. I want to keep looking because I haven't seen my guy flirting with anyone, and there is almost an hour left, and he could just be hiding until the very last song when he will pop out and find me and we'll both smile and blush and share a certain special, maybe silent, magic. I have this Disney faith in destiny and soul mates that is slowly slipping away from me, but I am trying to hold onto it by praying for him every night, like, *Please, God, gimme Jason I-Don't-Know-His-Last-Name-Yet-But-I-Want-Him*, and I think we are definitely meant to be together, because I've never loved someone this faithfully, for a whole entire *summer*, and if I just keep waiting and wishing on every shooting star I catch and every time I look at the clock and it is 2:22, or 3:33, and if I keep praying at night in bed in the dark with my eyes squeezed so hard that God must know I am serious, then something— something will happen to us. It kind of just has to. When she was nineteen at a college community potluck, a tiny voice told my mom that she would marry my dad, and I want this voice to whisper to me. I can't think of anything sadder than turning fourteen and not being completely in love and loved by him.

"Let's wait," I say. "It's almost over."

But she is gone. She saw an opportunity when the pink-streaked girl walked away to slip in. She's left me standing in the light by the entrance.

"Hey, where's your friend?" says someone directly into the back of my neck. My body stiffens because I'm scared I'm imagining things, but when I turn he is really, really standing there, with his hands in his pockets and his eyes all pools of blue and his head slightly bent toward his shoes like he might be in trouble. He has a silver chain looped from the back of his pants to the front and old white shoes he's decorated with marker. I'm staring down at them to avoid eye contact, cheesing and blushing.

"She just went to talk to someone."

I glance over at her but she doesn't see me. She's laughing, looks like she's telling a story. She is a soon-to-be-diagnosed compulsive liar who will get me in trouble one day.

"Awww," he whines. He just feels sorry for me. I stand on the outsides of my boots, looking at the singer, who's left the microphone now and is just jumping. "Well, c'mon," says Jason, "come with me," and he grabs my fingertips. We could be going anywhere but choose the maze. There are no lights set up inside, an oversight that could be dangerous, but right now I am grateful for the dark, and I walk so carefully in the ghosts of his footsteps, concentrating all my energy into the three fingers on my right hand that he is holding, so I can hold onto this feeling for a long, long time after he lets go.

My stomach is a mess. He looks back every few feet to smile and taste his lips at me. They are pinker and thinner up close. He is actually touching me, I remind and remind myself, and he's grabbing for my whole hand now.

"Where are we going?" I don't mean to sound scared of him but maybe I do.

"Don't worry," he says softly back. He inches his fingers up to bracelet my wrist for a second, then slides his palm into mine and our fingers lace. We've hit a spot where the moon glows through the floorboards above us. He's tall, and in the slow movement through blue light his hair looks shinier than that of any boy I've known.

But before he can kiss me we come out at the other end of the playground and he quickly releases my hand like he is dropping it off. He looks around before sneaking in his pocket for a cigarette and a Bic. He holds them out to me as an offer. I shake my head, sad that I don't smoke.

There is a tear in the fence that he goes through. He holds his cigarette between his teeth and uses both hands to pull the chain-link big for me.

There are people in a group back here. My heart pauses and sinks. One of them is a girl named Kat who is big-boned but gorgeous. None of them have dyed their hair. They are all sucking on cigarettes and sitting in a peaceful clump. He introduces me and I watch my name come out of his lips in smoke rings. I can't believe he knows it and how to pronounce it and I feel like fainting so I press against the fence and it bows out to fit my shape.

"Sit with me," he says, tapping a spot flat in the grass. But behind me my name is being shouted by the friend who left me.

I spin around and here she is, breathless. Her face looks oblong in the spot where she's standing between a shadow and the humming orange light from the pole.

"It's ten-thirty," she says.

We gotta go but I really, really don't wanna.

"I'll be right there," I whisper.

She looks at him on the ground and back at me. "Let's go," she says again. "Your mom's waiting."

My jaw breaks free from its sockets. I'm yelling at her in eye contact. "Gimme a minute," I speak through my teeth.

She rolls her eyes and runs off, probably to tell that I'm back here with a cute boy and he's a smoker. I don't want to turn back around.

Now he's already standing with a hand held softly on my hip. He gestures toward the rip in the fence with his hair and I follow him, burning. He opens it for me but doesn't come through. I look back and he lifts his cigarette as an excuse and an apology. Then he fingers for me to come close and we lean our heads on opposite sides of the cold black fence. He's still smoking, inhaling slow, blowing it out his mouth away from me. I know it is a disgusting habit, and inside his lungs are scorched, and we are surrounded by trees, and friends don't let friends start forest fires—but right inside this minute his addiction to lit tobacco is so sexy I feel sick. Our eyeballs are lined up. My brown could kiss his blue if we inched a little closer.

"You dyed your hair," he says. "How come?"

I shrug and don't have any answers.

"It looks cool," he says, and reaches into the small hole with a free finger to touch a green end. "But I think you were . . . like, even prettier? . . . before." He looks at the toes of his shoes after he says this, and kicks at the dirt. When he looks up again he's smiling so hard that the weight of it makes him drop his head right back down. And I want to soak in this moment, marinate, carry his sweet juices home. But I hear my name again, coming over the trees. I just know my mother is wearing some papery, bright authentic African dress against her white-white skin and feather-light, layered brown hair, and before this sight can get to us I tell him I gotta go. Sorry, sorry. I'm power-walking away toward her shrill sound.

"Hey!" he calls.

I stop and look back and he's stomping out his cigarette.

I wait for him.

He hesitates, then waves, and I run.

I know I am black, but I'm not sure what it means, and if it means bad things, like slavery and oppression and poverty, how to deal with it. Also, I do know I am white, but not really. Maybe for a while I thought I could choose a side to lean toward or on. But slowly, right in the middle of my punk stage, I come to understand that it isn't so easy to gain an all-access pass to either side, though black people in general tend to embrace you, while being white when you have a drop of anything else is one step from totally impossible. They don't just give memberships away, this is clear. There are grueling tests and probably fees I wouldn't be able to afford even if I wanted to buy my way in. Maybe I thought that because I was raised to speak properly, because I have never even dreamed of forming the word "nigger," not even with an "a" at the end, and because I've had a certain amount of exposure to light rock, and my brother and I play endless games of D&D, have an unhealthy obsession with the Middle Ages, and watch Monty Python movies back-to-back, because I ride horses and my mother is so white she is almost transparent and not even sunscreen can protect her, that we were just, automatically, admitted.

The hit comes sudden, in the summer between middle and high school, at Lollapalooza.

My best friend and I are standing in line for a Coke. In front of us is a tall white man, wearing all black except for his red bandanna, his sweaty forearm resting on the shoulders of a blonde. The back of his shirt is consumed in flames, and in the midst of them is a flag, loud and Confederate. I just learned what this symbolizes on a trip to Atlanta. And I just learned not to let anyone call me a mulatto, because it means mule.

The man is ordering beers and I am feeling faint reading his shirt again and again. It is a stern and confident warning: *The South Will Rise Again.* I read this and think that it might. And I hate him so much I want to tackle him. But I feel small and naked in the middle of the drunk, pasty crowd.

My friend rolls her eyes at him. "He's dumb," she whispers, but she didn't have to say that.

On our walk toward the stage to see Rancid I suddenly don't like white people or their stupid fucking music anymore. Not even my mother or my friend. I want to go hide under the dark arms of my daddy. There is another flag, its X of stars flapping in the wind, flying high over our heads, attached to a tent. On the other side of the tent waves one more flag with the wrinkled brown face of Bob Marley. I don't get it. Or want to anymore. I don't jump or clap for their songs or smile for the rest of the show. The first thing we did when we got there was stand in a long line to take a Polaroid with a chimp, named George like my father. He wore a striped-collared shirt and curled his top lip over his teeth when they told him to smile. Everyone wanted a shot with the monkey. I sit on the grass staring at the picture in the palm of my hand.

"They had a Confederate flag at the show," I whine to my mother. I think she will be appalled, jump to her seat, release a retaliation of phone calls. She just makes a disgusted face. "A *Confederate flag*," I reiterate. She nods, looking up over her reading glasses at me, not moved or surprised.

I rent the movie *Malcolm X* and watch it until my head hurts. I wish I could get my hair to hold an Afro but it can't quite. When I was nine my mother bought me an orange outfit made of kente cloth that I only wore once. Now I stare at it hanging in my closet, wishing it still fit or I had the nerve to buy and wear another.

"You like this movie," my mother notices. We are on our way to return it and rerent it all over again.

"Yeah," I say.

"So, are you ashamed to have the blood of the white devil in you?" She's smiling, filling the space between her joke and my answer with soft laughter.

I turn to the window and shake my head at her ignorance and do not respond.

Slavery has just slowed to a simmer, and black women are free to be beautiful again to a point. Not like they are in Africa, where kinky hair is the only kind in the world that grows toward the sun instead of the ground. In the obsession with making it straight they lose it. Now they are poor and pitch-black and bald. No one wants them on their arms or in their love shacks. They pick crops, scrub plates and floors and windows, hide in rags.

A woman experiments in a laundry room where she works, mixing a solution in stolen tubes and then selling it door-to-door. She makes millions and people can't stand her for it.

But she smoothes out the naps.

It's Christmas break and I am in a broken computer chair, facing away from the windows that look out onto the dark street. Jean has decided to play with my hair, now that the colors have washed out and the bleach can be trimmed away.

"Let me straighten it," she begs.

I shrug because I am supposed to be antiestablishment and anticonformity and antibeauty. But I can't go back to school in my Salvation Army clothes and baby barrettes. I am a freshman trying to keep new friends, the black cheerleaders. I don't want to be in a pep rally, but I am tired of trying to be white and badass all the time. I just want to be pretty. Plus I like a boy in my neighborhood who must think I'm dirty and insane.

So I let her do it, just a trial, no relaxer. She combs it out to an Afro, sprays and rubs grease into my thirsty scalp, which guzzles and demands more. My head has been needing someone to touch it. She runs a hot iron from root to tip and I almost fall off the chair, from the heat and the feeling of being loved all the way to the scalp.

When it's ready it has been hours and I am dizzy. She spins me around to face the window reflection of the metamorphosed me. It falls to my waist like a curtain. I'm suddenly cut from a whole different kind of material. I'm glossy now, so glossy that I reflect light in my hair. It sticks to the strands and radiates off. I stare and stare and stare and stare.

"I knew you were under there!" She's jumping on her tiptoes, proud of herself and her ability to make over. I can't stop cheesing. I don't even try acting like I don't love it.

My mom is here, honking, to get me. Before I leave Jean runs me upstairs to borrow her clothes: a tight pair of Levi's, two formfitting knit sweaters, Filas the colors of patriotism, a small puffy white coat.

"What did you do?" my mom gasps. "Tell me it's not permanent, please." Her hand hesitates like it's scared to touch, until I let her know it will only last until it gets wet. She sighs her relief. "Not that I don't like it," she lies, and now is able to pet. "Soft," she comments, and I smile because that is exactly what I've always wanted to be.

Girls whisper behind me in Biology. "Break was good to *someone*." This cracks them up. They slap hands over the insanity of their cleverness. One of them is huge like a grizzly squeezed into a toddler desk and the other looks like a dying bird, so they don't bother me. When the bell rings I get up and flick my hair behind my back, hoping it whips them. It's silky and feels plastic, like a prop, falling down to my belt. I sweep up my books and switch down the hall. I believe one of them directs a "bitch" at me.

I stand at a cheerleader's locker. She befriended me on the first day of school, probably because I was awkward and ugly. She is the type of cheerleader who only looks good from high up in the stands. She keeps glancing at me funny out of the corner of her eye. There are boys walking by my back but I'm too shy to look at them.

"Did you see the way he was checkin' you out?" she gasps. She shakes her head and slams her locker, holding a stiff smile.

"I love your curls," my mother whines. "I miss them." She has her fingers inside the long, shiny difference.

Jean comes over with a box of Dark and Lovely. If I do it I won't get more than a wave when it's wet. But I'm almost fifteen and need boys to look at me now. So we do it and it stinks and stings but then it is done and I have length and shine.

We toss my wardrobe back to the Goodwill whence it came. My mother surrenders her credit card for my first mall trip in years. I come back with bags and bags of the new me. I spin a lot now, and toss my head back and forth when I dance, get good jokes, and throw fits.

Every other lunch period a fight breaks out inside one of the long rows of chewing faces. Sometimes it's taken to a center where a cheering crowd can easily gather. A lot of times it only manages to climb on a tabletop. You never see it boiling before it erupts, not even if it is next to you. Not until you are violently shoved aside.

One time a pretty sophomore to my left gets interrupted in the middle of a bite. Her naturally long black hair is used to yank back her head before sending her face straight into the table. I jump up and stand back to watch like the rest of the room. Names are being chanted. The boys, especially, love it. It must be over one of them. Boys who skip class and can't even get out their mustaches. The only girls who scrap as violently as this are the ones who need the opposite sex like food and water, who maybe find a comfort in them like you might find in a worn blankie saved from babyhood. Even though the girl might not like the verb of sex, may actually hate the sight and smell of a penis.

The face-slammer is tall for a girl, wears glasses and a red weave in a French roll. This is grabbed for first. Fists fly and rip and screams echo off the high ceiling. The sophomore's hair is her own. It's pulled out and lying in bloody spots amongst the red synthetic pieces. The girls are going bald and wild. They call each other bitches and hoes as they tear up clothes and smooth faces. The bell rings and it is still going so no one will make a move toward class. Not even toward finishing or getting rid of their food. All eyes stare, entranced in the bloody passion of two girls who will soon be promptly suspended, and even weeks later when they return will never be forced into saying sorry by the principal, girls who will remember each other's names with a burn into adulthood.

The crowd is containing their chaos with its tightly formed circle of bodies. No one is chanting anymore, no one will dare to step in and break it up.

There is a girl standing at the front door of my boyfriend's house. She is actually the second one today. I just finished crying about the first one, who had bumps all across her forehead like land mines ready to pop you if you triggered them with a misplaced finger. She demanded to know if we were still fucking.

The three of us were standing on the concrete steps in front, inside of each other's personal bubbles. He laughed when she said this, then stopped abruptly and asked her who the fuck she thought she was talking to. "'Cause it sure as hell ain't me," he added, and I watched her slowly shut up. She is still in high school and probably new to him. She was scared to even look back up in his eyes. So she stomped off, then tires squealed on the asphalt, whined all the way through the weaving streets of the subdivision. He pulled me inside and consoled me all over on his couch.

Now I am staring from the safe distance of the living room at a girl who went to my high school, who walked a few alphabet letters behind me across the stage. So tiny and her weave takes up most of her. She has the voice of an annoying reöccurring character, high and whiny, and she is bawling because our boyfriend won't let her step inside to confront me with questions and, most likely, vulgar, rude comments. But even from the doorway she is screaming my name and I hate the way it sounds coming from her. She is pronouncing it right but still somehow butchering it. It is supposed to be Arabic and beautiful, but right now it sounds ridiculous and homemade. She's accusing me of being a light-skinned slut, goes so far as to call me a white girl.

"Think you so fuckin' cute," she chants. "Think you so fuckin' cute."

And he keeps calling her crazy, attaching it cleverly to various degrading nicknames. "You a crazy mothafucka!" he laughs. "Crazy ho! Crazy-ass bitch!"

"I know I am!" she screams. She just wants the shoes she bought him. So he deadbolts the door and races to his closet, comes back, and tosses a glossy box into her stomach.

"Take those fuckin' shoes, bitch!"

I cringe on the couch. When we ride around town in his Cutlass he pets me and plays all the cheesy songs I request, over and over if I want. He blows me kisses and holds my hand in public and even calls my mother by her last name. He doesn't threaten me with language or looks, has never even raised his voice at me. But somehow I knew he could do it. Could always picture, very clearly, him hitting a girl. His hands are not huge, but scarred and capable. She must know this. This is how he treats her and she isn't surprised. She melts into a puddle at his feet, pleading with him for the cordless phone.

"This ain't no pay phone service, bitch. Better take yo' ass down the street."

She's fuming, trying to push her way in, to rip her way past him with acrylic nails the orange of a ripe pumpkin. I just stood to see but now quickly step back and close my eyes. There is the shouting of her cartoon voice and his smoker's baritone. The burn of his sneakers on the sidewalk and scrape of her hollow heels. My stomach is churning, wondering if she might get inside. Trying to remember how many of those cafeteria fights she was in and if she ever won.

If she breaks past him this will be my first fight ever and I'll have nowhere to run except into furniture. Plus I have a lot of aggression toward him that I'll enjoy taking out on her small body. I won't know what to do but go for the fake hair. When she rips mine from my scalp it will hurt so, so, so much worse, but tossing her weave around his clean white living room will reveal which one of us is real and therefore prettier, better, and worth keeping.

But he picks her up and launches her off the porch, then slams and locks the door, leaving her outcast, irate, and crying. Slowly she circles the house, tapping steadily on all the windows and walls. Then runs around to the back and turns on the hose to soak his mama's lawn. When he shouts out that he's calling the cops she drives her army-green Neon up the street, parks, and runs back to hide in his bushes. She'll crouch for hours until someone points her out. He will storm out the door clutching a baseball bat, the real kind, solid and silver. He'll swing it and miss. She'll run off mascara-stained and wailing. A few months later I will be tearing and choking all over my dorm room, calling him again and again with no answer, and his daughter will be growing inside her miniature belly.

But before that: He is standing over me, and I can't even yell or make tears anymore. He laughs softly like an invitation to join him, but when I am silent he becomes that too. I want to run away from him like a troubled teenager from a dysfunctional home. I tell myself I am only still sitting here because I sense that she is out there and I'm scared that she will pounce if I try to slip by.

He reaches to touch my arms and I almost gag. Now I can cry again so I let it flow. "Don't do that," he says, "don't do that," but it's already done. He goes for me again and I shudder and make my body a ball. The only thing he can think to do is get me some Hawaiian Punch in a plastic cup. And lift it to my face slowly like nursing an injured animal, tip it down my throat, and step back fast from the bright red explosion.

He goes to the hall bathroom, screams, and comes back. He's standing in front of me in the perfect spot in this dark, empty living room, so that all around his figure the light from the kitchen glows like an aura. He's coming down on me with palms out like a parachute or a prophet.

"Look what she did to me," he says down my shirt. His voice is all over my neck, then just his breath, his lips, and his tongue.

"I don't care," I sob, but push him back to see.

He lets me shove him for the first and only time in our brief history and his face doesn't flinch or harden. He stands there drooping like the white flag for surrender, using the length of his eyelashes to pull me back on his side. He flips on the lamp next to me and tugs my eyes down with his.

"Just look," he begs, and is pointing.

She's dug deep red rivers all across his beating brown chest.

Sometimes, unexpectedly, a person, like a pretty girl in high school, can mysteriously start losing her hair. Shedding like it's the season. Leaving it around the house, on the coffee table, under the couch, in a sleeping boyfriend's curled hand. People find chunks of it and present them like long tubes of snakeskin that boys sometimes find in grass. Not only head hair, but body fuzz, everything. The eyebrows, the lashes, the pubes.

Just this has happened to a girl that Jenny knows through somebody else at their Catholic private school. The bald girl has been absent for a string of days. The rumor is that she'll never pop her head back into public. Supposedly her hair was blondish and nothing amazing. But another rumor goes that she's had a human-hair wig made that doesn't look at all like the long, silky original. And anyway, they can't fix the rest of her.

It's mostly for this reason that we are sitting at the Department of Public Health, filling out paperwork that asks us personal questions, like if we shoot or snort drugs, have we engaged in oral sex with another female and/or sodomy with a homosexual male. We check the boxes with our heads bent like tents. Glances are stolen at each other's sheets but the answers are boring. A guy we know is sitting across from us against the wall, rubbing his dry palms together. I can't stand it, the back-and-forth like someone walking through the room in windbreakers. I think he's probably always had parched palms. He's a mailman and near the height requirement for a midget. He used to like Jenny when she was thirteen and he was that plus ten carry the three. Once there was a phone fight between her and the insane mother of his baby. I remember he loved the screaming. He has jet-black waves and a grin with butter stains. Every once in a while he flashes his shiny black eyes at us to let us know he knows we see him. When his hand scraping finally stops it is silent in the room.

We would like to know whether or not we are dying slowly from AIDS. I'm pretty sure I'm in the clear but Jenny has been losing chunks of her long, natural red-brown curls in the shower. It has been sudden and painless. She fills the small bathroom wastebasket with the loss. Her hair accounts for a large percentage of her identity. Without it she would probably blend into a crowd at a busy mall or a parade and there would be nothing distinguishing enough to bring her back out. And this is true for me too. Without these wild spirals that tend to frizz in humidity it would be too easy for us to accidentally disappear.

After some research we have ruled out the condition that the girl from her school has, and the next logical explanation is this devastating sexual disease that she may have gotten from her dirty, dirty boyfriend.

We are rubbing our hands now, tapping nails on knees and jerking legs up and down without realizing. On the other side of the room is a woman who is burnt-blonde and stonewashed and fidgety like my idea of a whore. There is a man who looks asleep but has cracks in his small dark eyelids to spy. And a woman in sweats who looks like her feet would stink. The receptionists behind the cubicle are slaphappy.

"I don't wanna know anymore," Jenny whispers. She's next to me, sitting on her thin hands. We've already turned in our clipboards, been assigned numbers. Soon we'll give blood to a tube and that will be it. There will be no coming back to this spot in time when we don't know what's going on in our bodies. We aren't victims or survivors or lucky yet. After our results the world will look amazing or incredibly cruel. Either way we'll stop just trudging along. Up until this point we've reacted to most things with a shrug or at most a sustained chuckle. After this you can expect wild outbursts, tears, chairs thrown—small, un-choreographed routines.

But, "I don't wanna know either," I say.

We're subconsciously touching all the various levels of our hair, feeling for trouble at the scalp. Mine is thick and impossible to finger through as always. Really, I'm only doing this for support, to be the control of this group, but it's just hit me that I am actually scared to know. Anyone could have it and I don't want to have it. There is nothing that I don't want like this. I used to bawl watching Tom Hanks pretend to die. He won an Oscar that year or at least was nominated. My death wouldn't be as entertaining or noteworthy. It would be slow and smelly. The loss of control over my functions. I'd drown in my shit, my blood, and my spit, all bodily secretions collected in a smoldering pool underneath the sore-riddled remains of my body.

I float to the ceiling of this stale waiting room to look in on myself for symptoms. I see how tired I have been, almost unable to make it to work by eleven forty-five a.m., how pale I've stayed this summer. Without diet or exercise I am losing weight, rapidly; I know this because clothes have been slouching off me. My friend John, an ass expert, has been making fun of my recent lack of one.

I think of who might have given this to me, whose dick I will slit if the horrible news ever hits. Instantly I see a face. The round face of a bastard with really curly eyelashes and no regards for commitment. When I focus on his exact features it makes sense that I am probably dying.

"What will you do?" I ask Jenny.

It can't only be me. We'll both have it. For some reason we are smiling and trying to stop but can't help it. We have the same reaction when receiving long, confusing compliments from strange old men and/or lectures from authority.

She shakes her head at the carpet patterned with streets that intersect and dip and weave, something for the children pulled along to this place to kneel on, wishing they'd brought tiny race cars.

"Kill myself," she says. "I'd have to." She doesn't break her stare on the dotted yellow lines. I can see her vision getting blurry but she can't look anywhere else. I am growing panicked, glancing everywhere. I lean back and over a seat to take in all of her at once, to see if her hair seems proportionally smaller compared to her body. It does. Then it doesn't. It depends on how you look at it, what you think you should see.

Teenage boys come in, rowdy and embarrassed about the itch they have or how it hurts when they piss. Someone's given them something. Boys don't just come here. They sit behind us. Maybe they are worried about the same one we are. We could all have it. If so, we could form a support group. We could celebrate together during our final few years or moments. Maybe we could even break off into couples.

The mailman is called back. We think about running. I'm not ready because I haven't had time to decide if I will kill myself in a double-suicide with Jenny or be a spokesperson, visit Sex Ed. classrooms around the country, use my story to scare kids into condoms. "I was just like all of you," I'd say. "I never thought I could get this." If you have a terminal disease it's okay to be sappy; it's even encouraged, recommended, rewarded. I could enjoy that. I could be famous for how well I cope.

Jenny yanks out her phone and calls her mom. Carol works at the AIDS Care Network, where she specializes in stroking and listening to the victims of our tragedy. Jenny needs her last-minute opinion. I am now on the very edge of my chair, tipping.

"Do you think I might have it?" she whines into a cupped hand. "My hair's been thinning."

I hear a lot of stern consoling. I hear that hair loss is a sign of cancer not AIDS but Jenny should still get checked because that fucking Tony could have given her anything. I want to ask her mom about my future too but Jenny's number is called and she quickly flips her phone shut, jumps to attention. She walks away on the balls of her feet and sends back a help-less look for me to catch and swallow.

When it's my turn I hover aboveground the whole way through the doors and into the red folding chair. The woman who wants my blood is someone vaguely familiar, the mother of somebody I kind of know. She ties the long rubber string around my arm and readies her sterilized equipment quickly. "Okay," she says, and pricks my arm. We watch the dark blood leak out and rise in the tube and I am queasy, though not at the sight. She has a gold front tooth that looks solid all the way through and a raspy smoking voice that is soothing. All over her dark body veins are fighting to pop free of her skin.

I can't stand it. Not knowing and feeling like she can just glance at me and tell. She must see it in the color of my blood, splashing against the thin glass.

I ask if I can ask her something.

"Sure," she says.

So I ask about hair loss and weight loss. About if my fatigue is a sign. She gives a half-smile, says she's no doctor but to her I look fine. She says I would look sickly, greenish, if I had it. She offers to check my mouth for lesions and I open wide. She says, "Don't scare yourself, you look healthy," and my blood cells do victory laps around the internal track of my body.

I take this, her effortless opinion, thank her twice, and walk away with it, back to Jenny, who is waiting for me by the exit rubbing her Band-Aid. "We definitely don't have it," I gasp, out of breath without running. I tell her we would look an entirely different color, spotted, ghostly. She widens her eyes and pulls me behind her out the big double doors.

Outside our breath puffs white and she jumps up to strike the air like a basketball player who has scored. We are in the clear and clean, accord-ing to Rosy, or Rhonda, and I'm so satisfied with her conclusion that I won't even feel the need to come collect my results in ten days. Jenny will not follow up along with me. It was stupid, actually, to come. Waste of a Christmas-break afternoon. We won't be dying. Such a slim chance, almost in the category of absurd. So ha ha ha! We can look back and laugh, see that we specialize in being overdramatic, like everyone says.

We sit on our bare hands to warm them as the car purrs at a standstill in the empty parking lot. Snow is going to fall soon. The frost is here. I catch Jenny in the visor mirror, eyeballing her hair that even I can see has a little less stage presence to it. But whatever the cause she can slow the shedding by combing less frequently, getting some volume-enhancing products. I'll start eating less nothing, more protein, and invest in a multivitamin. Slowly I'll gain my energy, my missing body back. Nobody but the mailman has to know we ever came.

"You're sure she told you that?" she whines. She's touching the dull ends, gently strumming them.

"Of course," I sigh. "She said it."

I reach across to flip up the mirror for her.

She laughs.

We pull away shaking and chattering.

There are times, chunks of months, when I let my hair go natural. These periods are always triggered by the preference of a boy who wants something more challenging to run his fingers through, who wants the world to know that the girl in his passenger seat is at least part black, not as sleek and Asian as you might think when the hair is flat.

I don't cut it again, not ever. It climbs down the length of my back, grows against and into it like a garden wall, until the longest piece can touch the top of my ass when curly. It's so long and damaged that there comes a point early in my first year of college when I shouldn't even straighten it anymore because the straightness only exposes all the dry split ends. I don't want to give up my length or my sleekness. I just keep pressing it flat, sitting cross-legged in front of a small mirror propped by the wall, going over and over the tips until my arm hurts and I am surrounded by mist.

But it is also around this same time, in Chicago and on the edge of nineteen, and dating a man who loves himself and also for me to be anything but nappy, that I suddenly start not wanting to be processed. I rebel against his slick ideas.

Tonight when I come out curly, he sighs, whips out his phone to make an appointment for me to see professionals, twisting his back at me as he eases off the curb, speaking low like he is hatching a plot or surprise. I hate him and don't think he likes me much either. He's high-yellow and hairy and has small teeth. He disgusts me. But he drives a Benz truck and has VIP passes to the intricate world of Chicago celebrity. He thinks he is one of them but I know he is not. I am smarter than him and I know this too. I also know I am only one out of a plethora of girlfriends. But I cannot stop sleeping with him.

We are in his car, gliding fast down a shining blank highway, going somewhere or another—we are always going, going until gone. Even though it is not what he wants, he still leans sideways to stroke it while we eat our silent dinner of tiny White Castle burgers. He has his fingers in my mane and twists it around his short, stubby fingers, then a fist, pulling a little but not enough to hurt, maybe just to show how he could and just might. We are listening to the same sixteen bars of his sad and short-lived rap career, over and over and over again, over and over and over. Like always he has called me in advance to tell me an exact minute to come down the dorm stairs and also what to wear from my wardrobe and what to do with my hair. In general, he wants it to be as long and simple as possible. Doesn't want glitches, nothing that could catch on a ring.

We stop outside a club and I don't want to get out or go in. I pull down the visor mirror and focus on all my flaws. I threaten myself quietly that I'll cut, I'll make myself boyish and bald again. He leans over so he's elbowing my lap, and inside the small shiny rectangle we are both struggling to remain reflected.

"Cut it off and I'll cut you off," he says, then laughs. I join slowly and we are inside a mutual moment of uneasy laugher. When it trickles back toward silence, he says, "Naw, but for real, I don't like no girl with short-short hair." I stop my forced smiling and nod. He unbuckles my seat belt and motions through the window for the valet to open my door.

And maybe it is because I hate him so much and he hates my curls, or maybe because one time I iron it for him and my hand slips and the tip of my ear is burned; but just before Valentine's Day I give up on the hassle and hours of trying to stay straight. The short yellow man and his demands disappear slowly, fade wash after wash like a stain, and I only want him back a little bit. I cry about it to the girl in the mirror who has always been sad anyway, standing in the bright, open community bathroom of my all-female floor, and she bawls back and we feel very, very sorry for ourselves. Then we decide to stop. We will also cease the extremes of trying to be white, or even black, and form the beginnings of a friendship with what we've got.

So I abruptly put an end to the dying and hiding of it, try working through instead of against the mess, let it taste several types of mousse and sprays and defrizzers to see which one it prefers. Though it turns out to be none of them. And there are still years of tears over it. But finally, after a late-night reflection, comes a realization, or maybe it is something even better, something holier—a revelation—that my hair is probably the most opinionated part of me. I throw up my hands and step back from the mirror and all the tools and products lined under it, and I give it room to be big and loud and wild.

Church of the Living Womb Manifesto for Haters

by Liza Jessie Peterson

BREAKING NEWS FLASH!!!
RECENT MEDIA EVENT!!!

A headwrap-wearing, freedom-flag-waving, porch-monkey-puppet type working for a Miss Ann-type agent of conflama is reportedly running around slandering the name and reputation of Sistah Pastor Preacha Prayer, claiming Sistah Pastor Preacha Prayer done lost her mind and is having a nervous breakdown. Yes, Sistah Pastor Preacha Prayer did breakdown a lie and make certain power brokers nervous. Poor Little Pretty is confused.

Could Sambonita be making these false accusations? And if so, why?

Are house Negro rules still in effect?

You decide!

Here below lies the incident that brought all tongues to confess.

THE EVENT

The Church of the Living Womb was commissioned to participate in honoring Zora Neale Hurston on February 19, 2002. This event was to commemorate her latest released book of folktales, *Every Tongue Got to Confess*. This book had previously been sitting boxed in the bowels of European-American institutions (for over forty years) while Miss Zora lived her last years penniless and was buried in an unmarked grave.

Church of the Living Womb was asked to read several selected folktales of choice from her book. Upon choosing four very powerful and culturally affirming tales, it was then *strongly* suggested by one of the European-

American-controlling representative powers-that-be to read and close our ceremony with a "funny" selection about babydaddies.

> Preacher: Some got ten children waitin' in glory.
> Response: My God, ain't it de truth!
> Preacher: An' dey all got different daddies!"
> —"Preacher Tales," *Every Tongue Got to Confess*

Though this folktale does have its place in our rich tradition of signifying and playing the dozens, we felt it was not the piece to celebrate Zora's legacy and our culture. Nor was it the place—a packed auditorium, full of proud black people who had come to share in honoring a sister artist. *"Preacher: An' dey* all *got different daddies!"* Yes, family! This is what they wanted us to leave in the hearts and minds of our community.

So we, Sistah Pastor Preacha Prayer and Sistah Pastor Merlina, decided to let Spirit handle this arrogant, idiotic request. Addressing this social blunder at that time would only have taken us off our path.

How could they think they could dictate how we should honor our ancestor and how we should conduct ourselves in the context of our own culture and church service? In our church Spirit dictates sermon. So when Sistah Pastor Preacha Prayer channeled "Miss Z's Tale . . . Folk," a folktale divinely inspired by Zora herself, we knew it was a spiritual mandate that superceded culture-bandit protocol.

We work for the ancestors.

Power to the people!

We had church!

Sistah Pastor Elemental led the Church of the Living Womb in with song. We built an altar and collectively honored/acknowledged all of our ancestors with the congregation. We read scripture from Zora's new collection of folktales. Sistah Pastor Preacha Prayer continued the legacy of folktales, keeping the circle unbroken, by reading a divinely channeled new piece. Sistah Pastor Merlina acknowledged this momentous event by saying, "Yes, yes, seem like Zora still speaking through her children, seem like Zora's spirit still confessing."

Sistah Pastor Elemental led us out with song.

Yes, we had church!

Caught up in the excitement of the celebration, we left the stage before making an important announcement, so we returned. Sistah Pastor Preacha Prayer informed the congregation of CDs and books (including Tish Benson's *Wild Like That Good Stuff Smellin Strong*, and her audio excerpt, "Miss Z's Tale . . . Folk") on sale to ensure that artists (like ourselves) financially thrive while we are still living, not when our bones have turned to dust in the grave.

Church of the Living Womb was later accused of

1. hawking our wares (were Zora's wares hawked?),
2. "behaving in an unruly manner," i.e., reading ancestor text not under European-American domination, and
3. being disobedient.

The rotund European-American man-lady said, "Sistah Pastor Merlina, I thought we could trust you! We knew Sistah Pastor Preacha Prayer has anger-management issues, but *you* stood in my face yes-yesing to what we requested and turned around and did something totally different! The Church of the Living Womb is finished and will never be invited to any of our events!"

Sistah Pastor Merlina said, "No! Church of the Living Womb is not finished. We may not be invited to any of your events, but our ministry certainly continues!"

Rotund European-American man-lady said, "Well, I think I can speak for myself and my assistant [heretofore mentioned porch-monkey puppet] that this relationship is severed."

Sistah Pastor Merlina immediately communed with Sistah Pastor Preacha Prayer and asked her if she too heard the bells of freedom ring out. We don't ask for freedom, we snatch it, along with the hoods of culture bandits, exposing their banditry!

P.S. Because this Underground Railroad tactic has been vehemently challenged, questions come to mind. Such as:

1. What makes a real revolutionary?
2. If a revolutionary reveals her position to the enemy, is she a revolutionary or a fool?
3. Is the spook who sat by the door a dead concept in 2007?
4. Could an African-American dictate how Anne Frank should be celebrated?
5. How are we continuing the slave-massa relationship?
6. Do house slaves still exist?
7. Are there slaves who still protect the interest of the slave massa?
8. How do culture bandits hawk the wares and financially benefit from deceased black artists?
9. Should culture bandits dictate how African-Americans honor our ancestors?
10. Is freedom requested or snatched?
11. Do some Uncle Toms come cloaked in cultured garb wearing headwraps and dashikis?
12. Have we learned from the mistakes that our ancestors made in dealing with European-Americans?
13. If a headwrap-wearing, freedom-flag-waving Uncle Tom claimed to have the best interest of sistahs and thought Sistah Pastor Preacha Prayer was having a nervous breakdown, should she have (a) asked Sistah Pastor Merlina about it, or (b) gone around the community slandering her name with false accusations?
14. How can artists ensure that our work is seen, heard, and exposed while we are living?
15. Should the work of the living artist collect dust, only to later reap benefits after they are dead?
16. What is modern-day cooning and Tomming?
17. How does Miss Ann continue to stir up confusion and disorder in the black community?
18. How is Miss Ann keeping her slaves happy these days?
19. Are culture bandits still feeding off our ancestors?

20. Is having fearlessness and courage in the face of enemies a thing of the past?
21. What would Harriet Tubman have done to Tomming Negroes working for Miss Ann?

You decide!
Power to the people!
We shall continue to pray that the blind and misled will experience a spectacular awakening and remember their way back home.

Stay blessed and inspired,
The Church of the Living Womb

Email us:
Sistah Pastor Merlina: www.myspace.com/lizajessiepeterson

The Wu-Tang Candidate

by Miles Marshall Lewis

Dressed more like a punk vagabond than the hottest star of hiphop's new minstrel moment, Ace Boon Coon sits in full blackface makeup eating cold pork and beans straight out the family-size can. Reeking of the Salvation Army, his tattered Levi's are partially obscured by knee-high tube socks striped in red and white. The clownish colors show through the bottom of his worn-out Pro-Keds' gum rubber soles, which look a size too large for his feet. A snug, sloganeering T-shirt—*Axe me about my DUMB-ASS chirruns*—clings to his bird chest. Lint specks his unruly Afro. The beans aid in Coon's live show, six minutes to curtain, during which he infamously moons the crowd and farts loudly into a microphone held to his anus. Coon's publicist mentions he may have to redo the firetruck-red lipstick exaggeratedly circling his full lips. Slouched in a chair facing the mirror, he frowns, shakes his head, and lets one rip. A fecal rotten-egg stink assaults the marijuana-scented air of the Fox Theatre green room, coupled with his strong body odor. Coon hears a din of protestors outside the venue over the constant laughter of Richard Pryor's *That Nigger's Crazy.*

"Fuck 'em if they can't take a joke. I'm bringing that nigger style back to black music. Not 'nigga.' Nigger! Outside with their flyers and shit . . . They need to take a closer look at their history before they come trying to take money out of my pocket with their protesting. The minstrel style been in effect, boyee. Go get a late pass!" Coon says, ironically paraphrasing the politically conscious Public Enemy.

Ace Boon Coon applied his blackface hastily, after arriving late to avoid the contrarians outside. I ask him about his backstage blacking-up ritual and he laughs. "Ritual?" he asks. "Like a routine? Motherfuckers make me call off so many shows, I ain't even used to doing this shit yet." Wary promoters cancelled most of Coon's tour itinerary this summer, caving in to the pressures of protesters and civil libertarian groups including the NAACP. Most of his scheduled live performances end in ticket refunds. The rebellious atmosphere of a Coon show gives his occasional audiences the sense of participating in something anti–politically correct. Illicit. Naughty. The fact that crowds are ninety-eight percent white males doesn't faze him. "Busta Rhymes be rocking for just as many whiteboys as me," he says. "The whole hiphop shit is geared for them right now. This ain't the eighties, nigga." He breaks wind again, punctuating his point.

Coon's ritual-that-isn't starts with his pouring pure alcohol onto a few wine-bottle corks and lighting them in a large silver ashtray. He mashes the corks into black ashen powder, pouring in tap water to douse the flames. Protecting hands and face with cocoa butter, he spreads the resulting thick paste, slowly covering his own twenty-two-year-old boyish features, until the mask is complete. Lipstick comes last. To say the effect is spooky brings the old pejorative *spook* to my mind, as slanderous a term in its time as *coon* or *nigger*, to name two of this MC's favorites.

A blend of minstrel songs warms up the sold-out crowd: Ernest Hogan's 1890 smash hit, "All Coons Look Alike to Me," Lew Dockstader's "Coon! Coon! Coon!" These are interrupted once in a while by some modern tunes: Britney Spears's "I'm a Slave 4 U," Nirvana's "Rape Me." The weird mix finally ends, the lights die, and the boom-bap beat of "Pickin' Boogers" kicks off the show. The crowd roars.

Bubblicious and Risqué, both rising stars in their own right in the nearly soft-porn dominion of hiphop video, bracket the stage on either side. Wearing (if that's the correct word) itsy bitsy, teeny weeny, little polka dot bikinis, the dancers gyrate and shake mammoth saline-filled breasts and prodigious rear ends with vigor. If, like the star of the show himself, they're at all ironically subverting or merely flaunting stereotypes (of the oversexed black woman in this case), the effect is lost on the ogling fratboy crowd. Ace Boon Coon shuffles slowly out to center stage— barefoot, dully scratching his scalp—to more applause.

"Hey, Mom, what's for dinner?" he asks in his remixed cover of the Biz Markie rap classic.

"Go up your nose and pick a winner!" the audience yells in response.

Coon proceeds to do so, smudging the makeup around his nostrils with a finger and tasting some snot from his nose. Laughter floods the hall.

More kinetic percussion kicks in underneath a loop of the familiar ragtime theme to *The Little Rascals*, signaling Coon's breakout hit, "Black and Ugly As Ever." He drawls into the microphone: "I am product for a coroner / on the corner / Gambling my life / willing to throw to die / I got rope burns on my neck from noose / knots I done knotted myself tight / twined on tattoos." He emcees the chorus in tandem with a sample of Biggie Smalls: "Heartthrob never / Black and ugly as ever." Risqué claps her rear end to the thumping crunk, mirroring Bubblicious on her hands and knees. Coon joins in between them with his backside to the audience. He bends over, pulls his jeans past the crack of his behind, and expels noisy wet flatulence into the mic.

"Soundman, turn the music down," Coon commands. "I got a joke for y'all." The MC is known for his mid-concert funny story, always ethnically vulgar. On any given night the audience reacts variously—from nervous titters to uproarious fits of laughter—dealing with its suppressed opinions and attitudes about blacks (especially here, in an African-American-dominant city like Atlanta). "Why is the Wu-Tang Candidate, that nigga Hedley Dixon, about to lose the black vote in November?" Coon's never mentioned his political antagonist in public before, despite being vilified by Dixon since the beginning of his congressional campaign. "Nobody?"

"Blacks don't vote!" ventures a skinhead up front in a White Stripes T-shirt, to some laughter.

"Nice . . . True, we don't really vote. But the main reason we ain't voting for the Head Dick is, he's promising to create jobs for niggers!"

The crowd mulls momentarily, then cracks up.

The encore arrives ninety minutes later. The potent drum break and sizzling ride cymbal of John Cougar's "Jack and Diane" pulse hard through "The Nigger Ya Love to Hate," flavored with funky guitars from K-Rob and Rammellzee's "Beat Bop." Coon emerges from backstage with the cordless mic in one hand, a fresh watermelon slice in the other. He swiftly flaunts the trickiest rhyme flow he's shown all night. "Me, I sit in a rock-

and-hard-place state / festering hate / in the bowels of my abdomen / so evil that only harm to myself can ease the pain / I even reject my name . . ." Coon, sweat pouring from his blackface mask, munches on the fruit while an Ice Cube sample booms. He spits black seeds at the front row.

> From what he's told me of the hiphop culture, I can't see how his act is any different from what rappers have been doing all along. He says Snoop Dogg has a pornographic video series, the Beastie Boys used to inflate a humungous penis onstage, and his song about picking your nose is already twenty years old. I personally haven't seen his show but I'll never be anything but proud of my son.
> —Dr. Franklin Slader, Ace Boon Coon's father, July 2006

Malik Slader was born on March 1, 1984, into a middle-class family in Atlanta. His father, Franklin, was a highly noted authority on minstrelsy and remains tenured at Spelman, a local university founded for the education of young black women. His mother, Hawa, was an African lobbyist fighting against skin-bleaching creams proliferating in her native Ghana. Malik first began to emcee at twelve, writing rhymes imitating the cadences of his favorite rappers: Tupac Shakur, Nas, Biggie Smalls. His parents invested in recording studio software for his PowerBook and he came up with his first juvenile songs in high school, with titles like "Spit" and "Chocolate Box." Known as Lord Have Mercy, Malik changed his alias once another MC debuted on Elektra Records with the same stage name. Around this time an essay by cultural critic Stanley Crouch on the minstrel nature of hiphop, passed along by his father, inspired teenage Malik to bypass college and seek a deal as a rapper in blackface. Many labels expressed interest in his homemade music tracks and image, in spite of the inherent controversy, or, perhaps, because of it. Malik finally signed with Def Jam as Ace Boon Coon. *The Nigger Ya Love to Hate* sprang to the top of the *Billboard* chart the week of his twenty-second birthday. By summertime over three million copies rang through registers nationwide.

The Nigger Ya Love to Hate is a concept album for a genre unfairly judged as too dumbed down for concept albums. Ace Boon Coon may literally shuck and jive but the often-poetic lyricist tackles difficult questions of self-hatred, cultural appropriation, and the fine line between satire and indecency. Mainly self-produced, the seventeen-song album features guest luminaries Flavor Flav ("Niggerish Licorice"), T.I. ("I Got That Blacker Toast"), Trina ("Coons Use the Back Door"), and Southern chanteuse N'Dambi singing the chorus to "Strange Fruit (Watermelon Man)." Atlanta native sons André 3000 and Lil Jon both lend additional production. It's intentionally difficult to tell when *The Nigger Ya Love to Hate* spoofs hiphop and when it's deadly earnest, which is partially the nature of its success. "I ain't the first to do what I do," Coon opines. "Busta, Flav, Ol' Dirty Bastard—God bless the dead—Biz Markie, they all pioneered this. It's that clown prince style."

"We weren't the only ones ridiculed in playhouses during the minstrel days," says Gigi Martin, Ace Boon Coon's twenty-two-year-old fiancée, discussing blackface with grad-student fervor over Scrabble at The Beautiful, a soul food restaurant. The vivacious redhead arrived fashionably late for lunch, an entrance made all the more dramatic by her radiant beauty and smart style. The muscle-toned belly between her superlow-riding denim culottes and cranberry midriff hoodie flattens out past her hip bones to infinity. An L.A. native straight out of Brentwood, Gigi smiles movie-star-straight pearls (no doubt helped along by teenage orthodontics), curly locks grazing lithe shoulders, the bling of her diamond's cut just a shade away from ostentatious. She could be the thinner, younger sister of actress Lisa Nicole Carson; tiny pedicured toes peek through elaborately strapped Jimmy Choos. A Spelman College alumna, class of 2006, she enters Yale this fall for African-American Studies. Product of the American Minstrelsy 101 taught by Coon's father, she spouts knowledge from Dr. Slader's course fluidly. "In the early 1900s racism was equal opportunity. Vaudeville made fun of Irish, Chinese, and Germans too. Jews and Italians. People at that time expected their differences to be dissed. Dixon is just pushing the same old family-values button, trying to scapegoat Malik and avoid the real issues. Like the older white politicians." She sips lemonade.

Coon sits hiding behind sunglasses, lenses the shape and color of bugged-out Negroid buckeyes; today's provocative T-shirt features a forty-ounce bottle of Olde English malt liquor. He picks at an entrée of oxtails, chitterlings, collard greens, and fried chicken (all dark meat). Given Coon's youth and slightly bourgeois background, I wonder how much of his smorgasbord is an act for the benefit of this writer. Without makeup the rapper goes completely unrecognized—he's a young blue-black brother with a gorgeous girlfriend, like any other. A waitress bearing Gigi's garden salad fails to make him out. The Scrabble game proceeds with all deliberate speed. (Gigi's words: PHALANX, SYPHON. Coon's words: TRAP, BOOBOO.) He's been mum again on the subject of the Wu-Tang Candidate, but Gigi slowly draws him out.

The first salvo launched by congressional candidate Hedley Dixon involved an organized protest against Viacom for airing the salacious video to "Coons Use the Back Door" on *BET: Uncut* and MTV. The heavily YouTubed clip was already isolated to late-night airings for its graphic simulated sodomy; Def Jam voluntarily pulled the video from rotation after the resultant publicity boosted Coon's album back up the chart to number one. Antisodomy laws still stand in Atlanta and so Coon promoted illegal behavior, said Dixon. The *Atlanta Journal-Constitution* hence dubbed the thirty-nine-year-old grassroots activist "The Wu-Tang Candidate" (invoking the rap group Wu-Tang Clan) for highlighting hiphop in his bid for office in a way unseen since governor Bill Clinton roasted Sistah Souljah in the summer of 1992.

Scoring major newsmagazine exposure and a blooming constituency, Hedley Dixon pressed on, seeking a judge ruling to ban *The Nigger Ya Love to Hate* on obscenity grounds. A major platform point of Dixon's campaign touches on gender equality and ending violence against women, thus he pinpointed several sections of Coon's album for misogyny, sexual degradation, and obscenity violations. The ruling was denied based on a 1990s indecency trial concerning rappers 2 Live Crew and the Supreme Court; the First Amendment protects Coon's recording. Most recently Dixon has appeared on *Nightline* denouncing the depraved state of hiphop in general with Ace Boon Coon sighted in his crosshairs. Watching his sales soar as a direct result, the MC has maintained silence. Until now.

"All right, let's talk about Dixon," Coon says, crowning his bushy Afro with the unblinking darkie shades and sighing. "First of all, the man's an opportunist. That's real obvious. If his true problem was hiphop bringing down black people he wouldn't be fucking with me, he would be taking his beef to the corporations more. I ain't stupid, yo. I wear blackface. I know that pisses some people off. But I ain't the absolute Devil of the black community. Niggas were wearing iced-out platinum dental fronts and buying spinning chrome rims and other stupid-ass, wasteful shit before my album dropped. Dixon just wants to get elected. He ain't protesting Allen Iverson rocking conflict diamonds from Sierra Leone or Don 'Magic' Juan for marketing his life pimping hoes. I'm turning a buck how I see fit. This is America, nigga."

Speaking as a rapper, you think corporations are more responsible for what constitutes hiphop nowadays than the artists?

"Nigga, please. White kids buy hiphop! If my shit was some underground quote-unquote 'positive rap,' I wouldn't even sell a hundred CDs. Who buys shit like that outside the Zulu Nation? Corporations put power behind what people buying records wanna hear. The minstrels sold white people's craziest ideas about niggas back to them for entertainment back in the days, and that's what the most popular hiphop does now. I'm just blatant about it, and I'm fucking blowing up off it."

"Malik and I debated this all the time when we first met," says Gigi. "I totally agree with him now. 50 Cent is popular for fulfilling this über-Negro role for suburban white kids: shot, jailed, unstoppable. My parents collect Negrobilia, like the mammy cookie jars and stuff? They believe in reclaiming racist images, taking the power away from the whites who put it out there. Malik's very smart. If we can reclaim the N-word, then why not the minstrel tradition? If we pocket the spoils, then the joke's on who?"

No, I haven't followed Dixon's campaign remotely. We're registered Republicans in this house.
—Dr. Franklin Slader, July 2006

Across Auburn Avenue from The Beautiful stands the brick temple of Ebenezer Baptist Church. Martin Luther King, Jr. was baptized and later delivered Sunday sermons here during the civil rights era. Spacious grounds dedicated to the preacher's legacy stretch a couple city blocks' length behind the characteristic Southern church, including an eternal flame and Dr. King's tomb, elevated in the center of cascading waves of water. On a breezy Thursday, days after watermelon dessert with Ace Boon Coon and his fiancée, I return to the historic neighborhood to rendezvous with the Wu-Tang Candidate.

Informal polls show Hedley Dixon leading the race for Georgia's fifth congressional district. The young nominee has never held office of any kind but his widespread grassroots activism is locally known. Most recently Dixon spearheaded a fundraising drive for victims of Hurricane Katrina at Club 112, filling a literal truckload (said truck parked in front of the nightspot) of clothes, donated furniture, and canned goods to be driven directly to Louisiana. Until two years ago citizen Dixon was known as Hedley X; the young Muslim minister has been estranged since 2000 from the Nation of Islam—the cauldron of seminal black political figures like Malcolm X and Louis Farrakhan. In 2004 he reclaimed his given name and put together an informal exploratory committee to gauge his chances of getting elected Congressman Dixon. Like campaigns of the Reverends Jesse Jackson and Al Sharpton before him, this run should allow Dixon to leverage his political power more concretely, whatever its outcome.

Shaking hands he immediately chastises me for writing this profile instead of a damning editorial. "Frederick Douglass, a forefather of the journalism you do, came out strongly against minstrels in his day. It's bigger than hiphop, brother," Dixon says as we walk the distance of the King Memorial. The Wu-Tang Candidate says *brother* a lot, the way young white teenagers might say *dude*, or blacks of different eras have used *homeboy*, *yo*, or simply *man*. The way Ace Boon Coon uses *nigga*. "Yes, I grew up with the culture, I'm one of the first to take it for granted. I know my Run-DMC, 'Roxanne, Roxanne.' I remember Latifah when she was just a teenager! But I consider hiphop the voice of the young black community on a whole, not only rap music. I've been trying to take the conversation away from Brother Slader and talk about some of the bigger issues: education, self-respect, reparations."

The Nation of Islam in his past, Dixon still carries the conservative air of the famously bowtied believers. His Caesar is neatly shorn, pinstriped suit pressed like he hasn't sat all day, shoes spit-shined to a glow. He rests at the head of King's crypt as if predicting the photo-op. "I have no personal bias against Brother Slader," he says. "But he's the perfect lightning rod to draw attention to the fact that black folks' values in this new millennium have become sorely misplaced. This brother believes he can traffic in minstrelsy—one of the most egregious affronts to the dignity of blacks in American history—and profit from it without a problem? I've got a problem." A Lexus glowing neon-red underbody lights hairpins the corner, its deep-bass sound system vibrating the windows of the King Memorial with Coon's "Niggerish Licorice." The car floats down Auburn like a hovercraft; Hedley Dixon shakes his head.

Dr. Franklin Slader welcomes me to his new home in affluent Buckhead the next day. (Elton John and Ted Turner are neighbors, but this elegant four-bedroom Colonial is dwarfed by their nearby mansions.) Frames adorn the marble fireplace mantle, portraits of the MC as a young man: private school graduation; a summer spent abroad with grandparents in Accra, Ghana. Mrs. Franklin Slader, née Hawa Kiwojolo, makes an arresting appearance both in photos and in person toward the middle of our interview. Scarred from hydroquinone lightening lotions, her skin—most noticeably her face—is severely depigmented, irregular pink patches breaking up her natural coal-black tone. Listening to Hawa discuss blemishes resulting from creams used to lighten her skin, the irony of her son's use of blackface to darken his own comes to mind. How will his scars manifest one day?

Hawa Slader refuses to speak of her son's rap career but she does talk about her past experience with products designed to retard her melanin. Cultural prejudices about the superiority of lighter skin rampant in the African capital of her birth caused her and a good part of the population there to abuse hydroquinone creams. She gradually suffered blotchy puffiness and splotches; eventually a permanent melasma condition set in. Throughout the late-nineties Hawa successfully lobbied her home government to ban the sale of these harmful carcinogens. Dr. Slader helped draft her speeches. The connecting thread between a mother discolored from lightening her skin and a son who makes millions by blacking up is something Professor Slader also refuses to explore out of respect for his wife. He's understandably much more comfortable talking about Ace Boon Coon, the reason they're entertaining me in their home.

"I see Malik playing a character," says Franklin, "a modern-day variation on Jim Crow. Two of the greatest pioneering minstrels from the 1800s were white men using the stage names Jim Crow and Zip Coon. The flashier of the two was Zip Coon. He replaced buttons on his vests and coats with gold coins that he'd fling out at concerts. He reminds me of today's rappers obsessed with platinum jewelry and diamonds. He was more a caricature of the Northern Negro. But Jim Crow preceded Zip Coon, and his style was a distortion of the Southern country field Negro. Zip Coon wore high hats and tails with gold-coin buttons, but Jim Crow had holes in his shoes, clothes all tattered up. His hit record "Jump Jim Crow" made him the first international superstar of minstrelsy. That's who I see when I look at Malik's CD.

"I'm no apologist for the minstrel tradition, young man. But it's impossible to critique something you don't know the full history of. I assume you're here to critique Malik fairly."

The professor teaches class: "When the freed slaves performed in blackface after the Civil War, some of their minstrel songs included antislavery messages. These blackfolk were not sellouts! Blacks had a hand in creating the minstrel tradition from the absolute beginning. Why shouldn't we have taken advantage of traveling the world and making a living off what we helped build in the first place?"

Ace Boon Coon arrives, entering the den hand-in-hand with Gigi and his mother. Like backstage at the Fox, Coon looks less poor than punk: ragged Levi's; distressed combat boots; a Buckwheat T-shirt underneath a frayed jean jacket. His hair is matted like he rolled out of bed a minute ago. Gigi is his polar opposite, habitually glamorous in a tight baby-T (reading *Boys are stupid, throw rocks at them*) with a madras miniskirt and open-toe stiletto pumps. "Sorry we're late. Colored people's time, huh?"

Conversation wends around to the election once more and Malik Slader defends his Ace Boon Coon alter ego against Dixon for the final time. "Why can Shyne be Shyne and I can't be Coon?" he asks, invoking the jailed former protégé of Sean "Diddy" Combs. "To be called a shine used to be just as offensive. But nobody ever mentions that with him.

"Look, a lot more black people got jobs because of me than Dixon got scrambling around trying to get into politics: my publicist, my road manager, my personal manager, my accountant, my lawyer, my stylist." Gigi giggles at her ragtag fiancé mentioning a stylist. "For somebody bringing down the race, I'm sure creating a lot of income for the community. On Def Jam too, a record label created by a black man and run by another black man. The fans love what I do; I sold over three million CDs. Who picked that Nation of Islam dropout to decide what the black experience is and isn't allowed to look like? My audience laughs *with* me, not at me. I'm a millionaire, yo. These whiteboys don't seriously think I fart around all day long eating watermelon. They grew up with just as much love and respect for hiphop as we did.

"Remember that KMD record, *Black Bastards*, with Sambo on the cover hanging from a noose? That was over ten years ago. Fans been sophisticated for a long time, don't take away their choices. Why can Ludacris drop an album called *Chicken-N-Beer* and I can't do my minstrel satire? Dixon ain't calling out Ludacris, and he's right down here in Atlanta with us. Dixon's a hypocrite. No further comment."

For all his talk against the excesses of young black culture, Hedley Dixon demonstrates the same excesses at his election-bid benefit. Were the *Bronx Biannual* reporter still in town for this political networking soirée instead of long-since headed north to his native Brooklyn, he'd be using his journalistic senses of sight, sound, smell, taste, and touch to capture Compound in all its glory this Saturday night. Dixon's party looks like nothing so much as a rap music video: attractive blacks dressed in Armani and Sean John, Moshood and Gucci; a few celebrities sprinkled throughout—Coca-Cola chairman E. Neville Isdell; local record producer Jermaine Dupri with girlfriend Janet Jackson; Morehouse president Walter Massey. Free drinks, dancing, flirting. Dixon's party sounds like 2006 R&B hits from the hand of the regular weekend DJ. Dixon's party smells *hot*, the rising heat of too many bodies pressed together when it's still eighty-seven degrees outdoors at eleven-thirty at night; eaux de toilette, oils, musk, funk. Dixon's party tastes like sour apple martinis courtesy of open bar liquor sponsor Absolut, secondhand cigar smoke, the acrid tang of naked ambition. Dixon's party feels like America is about to have a congressman who knows his Run-DMC.

Thoughts sprint a marathon through Dixon's brain as sycophants glad-hand him every ten steps, hoping to add even more to his mental race. In his mind a teenager wearing a kente shirt with a red, black, and green leather medallion of Africa swaying around his neck riles up undergraduates on the steps of a college administration building. A natural ham, a born public speaker, he impresses the student body with knowledge he only just learned himself in the past few months—blended theories from Frantz Fanon, Che Guevara, Huey Newton, Chuck D. Other freshmen and sophomores from the dorms are behind him, behind the locked doors, holding the offices hostage. For the rest of his term at Morris Brown College, well after the building burns down in an unrelated faulty wiring accident, well before faculty force him to withdraw, the Atlanta University Center knows young Hedley X as a handsome rabble-rouser sharing the same fiery, demagogical spirit as his revolutionary heroes. A professor from those times now chairs a committee to raise funds for the school, which lost its accreditation some years ago and currently struggles with an enrollment of little over fifty students. How will Congressman Dixon help? he asks.

Another thought competing with the plight of Morris Brown is Zoraida, behind a velvet rope chatting up a rapper oblivious to Dixon's hiphop vendetta. Little Jamal is asleep in Greenbriar with his grandma; Dixon didn't expect Zoraida to attend but here she is, scarcely fitting into that favored silk scoop-neck dress. The mother of Yusufu would never have come. He'd hear from Kerisha soon enough if he won the popular vote, he knew. He knew just as well that Zoraida's turquoise scoop-neck wasn't for him, it was to remind him of what he messed up, the good thing he was missing out on. His conviction was equally strong about the reasons for his attraction to Gigi Martin, that she resembled a younger Zoraida: bubbly, brainy, hiding a hint of something hard to put your finger on, something devious. Angelic devilishness. Dixon thought of their appointment tomorrow and wanted to see Gigi tonight, wanted her here at Compound, the possible danger an aphrodisiac of its own.

Memories of his mother won't leave Dixon's head lately either, even here, recurring as often as old arguments they used to have over the Nation. Meeting a security officer from the Fruit of Islam underneath a shady highway crossing near the Omni Coliseum, he remembered her. Her voice came to him in these moments; she would've been proud to see her son's strides. She told him tales of mob ties; harassment her friends suffered in the sixties for failing to sell enough *Final Call* newspapers; the problems former convicts went through eventually trying to leave the organization; Brother Malcolm and his tapped telephones, the Honorable Minister and his babies. Times had changed, the hardheaded son countered, even if any of what his mom said was true. Near the Omni, by dilapidated shacks habitated by the homeless, Dixon dealt with an FOI brother talking about guns, airplanes, hotels, beaches, plans, and schemes. And about those shacks? asks an activist in a sky-high headwrap. How will Congressman Dixon help the dispossessed?

Ace Boon Coon has one week to live. Only Hedley Dixon and a rogue in the black Muslim militia know this to be true.

Secrets are sexy. Malik puffs herb past midnight alone in his high-rise apartment building now and again, spending his night downloading videos featuring Risqué, exciting himself with knowledge nobody else has. As much skin as she shows the world, people still don't know about the cashew-shaped birthmark on the heart side of Risqué's ribs. Schoolkids who vote for "I Got That Blacker Toast" on MTV's *Total Request Live* don't know that Ace Boon Coon's dancer likes to beat her fists lightly on her lover's chest in bed; that her legs go numb after sex, or that she still retains sensitivity in the tips of her breasts despite the saline engorgement; that her G-cup is a size smaller than her partner Bubblicious's. Malik knows. Sometimes she'll call in a record label car service voucher, get chauffered downtown to Marietta Street, share his weed, and fuck the notorious MC till sunrise. Even more so since Gigi matriculated at Yale.

Malik and Lakeisha suffer rug burns on their knees from the teal carpet of The Raleigh, moving and moving four-legged across the floor chasing climax. They laugh aloud about their lovemaking scars afterwards, lounging in the king-size bed of their suite. Lakeisha rolls over the luxurious bedsheets and plush pillows, laughing inwardly at the spoiled peroxide redhead she once envied for so many reasons. The November night sky of Miami softly illuminates the room while Malik rolls marijuana into a White Owl.

"If she wasn't gonna get 'em done, why she come to the audition?"

"She thought I was playin'? Jana spoke to some of them after. A couple said they ain't think the implant thing was for real."

"I wonder about her sometimes, since. If she wasn't so shook I wouldn't be here."

They'd reached a new stage in their relationship, the stage where a couple discovers feelings for each other beyond the sex, and now they lay together naked considering everything leading up to this beachfront hotel. Discussing future concerts with a musical director before releasing his album, Malik's most inflexible idea involved a go-go-dancing duo shaped like twin Jessica Rabbits. Parody trumped allure, by design. Malik auditioned professional dancers and career strippers with implants willing to submit to even more extreme enlargement. Not for desirability; for absurdity. Tico and Marlene quickly outpaced competition, but in the end, Marlene—somewhat known from a reality TV show—refused to give her body over to Malik's perverted idea of performance art for a six-month touring schedule. After surgery Tico quit Magic City and started lining up work starring in raunchy rap videos as Bubblicious. In lieu of Marlene, Malik chose the runner-up he'd most want to fool around with on the road, a twenty-one-year-old from southwest Atlanta.

"Am I too heavy?" Women pose this question because of Malik's small frame, but, actually, not all that many women have asked because Malik hasn't slept with all that many women. Everything is relative, his father always says—at the age when prep school girls were rejecting Malik because of his skinny body and ink-black complexion, Lakeisha was dealing with the flirtation of strange men bringing hard drugs to her mother's apartment. Use what you got to get what you want, she advised her only child, leading by example. Malik has always been thin but Lakeisha's mother emaciated gradually, even as her daughter's womanly frame continued to fill out. Malik directed his misfit rage into emceeing; Lakeisha turned the anger over her mother's young death inward.

"I love you on top. Don't move," he says, cracking joints in his feet with his toes. Malik's flighty engagement to Gigi didn't matter to Lakeisha, her last man was forty and married; an opportunistic fiancée wasn't cause to slow her roll. Malik—a newly rich celebrity—felt increasingly powerless to turn down sex or prevent himself from chasing it, with such a recent history of rejection and accumulated hostility over being ignored by impossible prospects like Lakeisha and Gigi. He proposed to Gigi in St. Martin after a passionate months-long relationship full of all the pent-up, unexpressed love he'd never been able to share, at least not with the type of woman he'd always wanted. A fling with Lakeisha—after many teasing rehearsals watching her practice strip-club moves with Tico—was even more exciting with the added aspect of keeping it secret. (Or was it getting caught?)

Secrets beget secrets, as more mature lovers already know. As of this feverish Saturday night in Miami, Malik has yet to learn about Lakeisha missing her menstrual cycle two months ago.

Gigi Martin rides a late-night flight from JFK to Hartsfield skimming *The Virtue of Selfishness*. Before landing she goes through the *Bronx Biannual* feature on her fiancé again. She'd felt the writer was attracted to her even at the time; she considers her suspicions validated rereading his fawning descriptions of her: *gorgeous*; *glamorous*; *radiant beauty*. Gigi's tried offsetting her looks with natural tomboyishness all her life, yet boys and men never seem to pay attention beyond her pleats and platforms, beads and bangles. Gigi, sitting on twin mattresses in dorms of the all-male college nearby her alma mater, has belched in front of guys and still watched them discreetly adjust their crotches in suddenly cramped jeans, laughing off her supposedly innocent crude behavior and turned on by it at the same time.

She only packed a carryall for her weekend in Atlanta; she intends to do Rodeo Drive with Malik when she arrives in Miami. Departing first class she rents a cart to roll her baggage on. After three months in New Haven, the events of the past year don't seem quite real to Gigi anymore. Her hallowed Ivy League halls have certainly known their share of conspiracies, but Yale's latest Af-Am major surely contributes a worthy addition to the storied university this fall. Critics complaining that modern-day hiphop has all the integrity of wrestling still couldn't imagine the covert pact between Ace Boon Coon, the Wu-Tang Candidate, and grad student Gigi Martin.

"Hi, I'm going to West End? Claremont Drive, West End Apartments?" The cab driver activates her meter and hurriedly pulls off in silence.

She wants to be rid of the whole cloak-and-dagger affair she helped concoct a year ago now; the scheme seems to be turning a corner, getting greedy. Things worked well enough up till this point. Hedley got the attention he coveted, the *Nightline* and *Newsweek* interviews, September's victorious primary. Malik sold millions of extra records and scored immeasurable currency in controversy with the national spotlight trained on his minstrel antics, pumping some of his profits back into Hedley's campaign in appreciation. Gigi alone objects to this fake death threat as wholly unnecessary. Staging an Election Day assassination attempt on Malik's life à la Big and Tupac will add even more to the mythology of Ace Boon Coon, but the fallout could sabotage them all should something go wrong, and so Gigi can't understand why Hedley came up with it.

For the first time in their complicit plotting Hedley's flirtations have become blatant, and lately the politician seems almost condescending, like he's dealing with a kid. The downtown skyline speeds by out of focus as Gigi stares through the window struggling to concentrate on one thought at a time. Would she fuck Hedley? she wonders. Arriving at their (hopefully) last clandestine meeting place—Hedley's home—will she sleep with the soon-to-be congressman if he has the nerve to proposition her? Gigi knew Malik fucked groupies, of course he did. It wasn't something she'd normally tolerate, but she felt certain their relationship would never really evolve to the altar. Gigi's self-awareness included an intimate knowledge of her own shallow side—a side that couldn't refuse a reputation among Spelmanites as fiancée of a rich and famous rapper. He proposed; marriage to Malik wasn't *her* intention. The rise and fall of Ace Boon Coon would crest within three years, she'd thought from the start, two albums, maybe three. If they married and Malik could adjust to a formerly famous life, she'd be seeking tenure somewhere by then, and with their money properly managed she'd gladly stick by his side. In the face of an uglier outcome, she'd be entitled to millions as a result of his infidelities, a card she'd no doubt be able to play whenever she wanted.

Malik and Hedley avoid all direct contact with one another; can she sleep with Hedley? Does she want to? For the briefest of moments a luxe future involving a husband in the House of Representatives flashes through her mind.

Gigi arrives at the apartment complex, pays her fare, climbs the town house steps, and hands Hedley her leather duffel when he answers the door. She removes her Lacroix boots and conducts straightaway business: Malik wants blanks fired, wants to know exactly when to expect the shots, wants a specially coded text message sent to his pager in the event of anything unexpected. Hedley, listening intently across a coffee table, opens a bottle of rosé and responds in turn: at high noon a gunman will open fire harmlessly on the closed set of Malik's beachside video shoot and disappear without a trace. He'll need the same access pass as the rest of the crew, Hedley says, passing Gigi a fragile, bulbous wine glass. Between her second and third refills of Domaines Ott, she decides whether or not to give it up.

Ace Boon Coon wears a black tuxedo and bow tie on Miami Beach, his normally choppy Afro blown out; highwater slacks show off sequined silver socks. Director Benny Boom's concept is to outfit Coon as Michael Jackson from *Off the Wall*, his regular blackface intact. All involved hope the media will eat up the irony surrounding whitefaced Jackson parodied by a black-faced minstrel. With every take, "Black and Ugly As Ever" echoes across the beach, Risqué and Bubblicious gyrating per usual, Coon rhyming into the camera over his own background vocals. Gigi looks on nervously from the boardwalk. At the stroke of noon she doesn't spot the gunman but still hears his muffled silencer. She can't turn her horrified eyes away from the wide arcs of blood suddenly staining the sand, can't stop the screams leaping from her gut as she dashes to Malik, fighting past a tanned horde of women in bikinis running in the opposite direction. Lakeisha reaches him first, crying on her knees, Malik in her arms. No one thinks to cut the playback of the *Little Rascals* theme.

The Wu-Tang Candidate wins in a landslide.

(Special thanks to muMs the Schemer for all Ace Boon Coon lyrics.)

The Egg Man

by Sun Singleton

Fruit pancakes weren't Malik's specialty. And yet, as a former wrestler with alpha-male drive, Malik considered himself a demi-master at most of the goals he pursued. That included cooking egg dishes. He could rock an omelet. He knew his way around the sunny-side up, the over easy, the Benedict, the Florentine, the occasional Croque Madame. He cooked those motherfuckin' eggs like he was infusing them with the power of his lust for his statuesque mahogany love, Tamoyo. The rye toast with just the right amount of crisp on the edge, and the perfect melt of Gruyère cheese, no bubbles, over a yolk that, you know, you pierce it with your fork and it bursts in all directions like sunlight from behind white clouds.

Yes, Malik was an egg man. Not a pancake man, and definitely not a got-dang fruit pancake man. Some cats actually know how to make sense of the lumpy banana mush and wet blueberry nuggets . . . so messy, this whole business. But Tamoyo was all about some fruit pancakes, so if diffusing her mysterious anger meant that Malik would have to step into this foreign terrain of breakfast, then so be it. Dude turned a chocolate suede paperboy hat backward, pulled up his sleeves, and dove naked hands into the bowl of raw banana. He smashed the three bananas between his thumb and index fingers, and sucked his teeth with disgust when he felt the cold meat lodge under his fingernails. "This has got to fucking work. I'm not good when she's not good," he implored to the God of Pancakes, who might trigger a warm sugar high in his lady.

Tamoyo was angry about something; he knew this because when she awoke this morning, at exactly six-thirty, she slipped out of bed without that first sloppy kiss that jump-started his day. He missed his pillow woman, and the sight of her coconut booty quivering softly under the lace of lavender boy-cut briefs as she rose out of bed. In fact, her soft brown lips were his coffee. He even missed her faint oniony morning breath. Tamoyo slipped into the shower like a ghost this morning, and he heard a despondent Sade song playing on the box in the bathroom.

The arguments between them had been particularly ferocious this month, the Christmas holidays always managing to inspire a mood of chronic dissatisfaction in Tamoyo. She complained about the apartment being too small. They shared a one-bedroom in Prospect Heights that Malik once had all to himself, until a year ago this past Sunday. With Baz, his furniture-design partner, out of town for the week, Malik had to cut and build table models alone, so he came home a dog-tired shell of his normal self. But rain or shine, a screaming match with Tamoyo always awaited him.

She'd gripe about little repairs around the apartment that remained broken for "an eternity," oozing melodrama. Malik felt like a scolded child, so he left the faucet dripping. He always had the nagging sense that Tamoyo was saying one thing but really talking about something else. It became like a code between them. Temp jobs always left Tee funky at the end of the day, and stories of drunk bosses hitting on her were endless. Complaints about the apartment often seemed to boil over after Sunday afternoon chats with Tamoyo's mom turned sour. Ma Jean was the type of matron who could enter the home of any person—friend, foe, or complete stranger—and call out the sight of a dust bunny under the kitchen table with a sharp sucking of perfect ivory teeth and the utterance of her favorite expression: "Clearly, nobody in this house has any damn home training!" But there hadn't been any call from Ma Jean over the weekend; Malik knew this because Tamoyo was usually quite verbal about the things that bothered her, even as Malik hid behind his laptop and half-listened to most of it. But today, absolute silence. Malik didn't know what to do with Tamoyo's quiet, it was nowhere in his knowledge of her code. Her silence was like a slow-working poison on his guts. His stomach was actually cramping. Without information, Malik felt like a lost child. So he went back and pulled a memory of Tamoyo squealing over fruit pancakes.

"Pookie! How many ways can you cook an egg? I feel like something sweet for breakfast today." She would pout as she said this, and it was so cute to Malik. He loved to see her pout, it meant she needed him.

"Okay, love, I'll surprise you with a treat then." And with a wooden spatula, he'd go to work mashing bananas and pouring honey into batter. Delicately, he'd lay each silver dollar–sized pancake down before Tamoyo. She'd bite into a forkful of the crispy sweet, buttery thing and smile. A mixture of calm and euphoria would wash over Malik like a good cognac high.

He hoped for Tamoyo's smile to blossom again this morning, prayed for it to happen even, and placed a stack of fruit pancakes on a gold straw-woven placemat. He added a few slices of red strawberries for the color of love and soaked the plate in a wave of dark maple syrup that pulled the strawberry slices under completely, drowning them in sweetness.

Malaika Descending

by Sheree Renée Thomas

I went to visit my Aunt Malaika, in Hell. The bus took so long to get there, I started to give up, tell them to let me off so I could go home. Seem like we wasn't doing nothing but driving around in circles no way, and all I could think about was, *Aunt Malaika gone, Aunt Malaika gone.* She had died about six weeks earlier, slipping on the wet pavement on her back porch and breaking her hip. They say she lay there, her wispy braids resting in her white rosebush, the thorns pushing up in her eye, until her half-blind neighbor, Ms. B., looked over the fence that separated their back-yards and called an ambulance.

Of course, they were late.

It took them two hours to come. "Ain't no hurry," somebody heard them say. "The old heffa already dead." I guess there was no secret about folk not liking my Aunt Laika. I can call her that now, since she gone. She can't do nothing to me no way—not with her being in Hell and all. Because if she could, Aunt Malaika would have slapped the taste from my mouth, would have had me reciting scriptures until I was hoarse and the black ran down my face.

Because everybody know that Aunt Ma-la-i-ka don't like nobody "skimping on her God-given syllables," messing up her melodious name. You got to say four—*Ma-la-i-ka*—or don't say it at all.

Everybody know that—at least *most* everybody.

The last time somebody messed up and called my aunt "Miz Laika" instead of her navel name, Ma-la-i-ka, she killed them. Actually, she let their daddy die, but that's killing all the same now, isn't it? That was one of the last times somebody had to call the ambulance to Alma Street too, and it was poor Raybone who ended up knocking on the wrong neighbor's door.

His daddy, Mr. Wilder, lived two shotguns down from my Aunt

Malaika's house, on the other side of the street, and apparently Mr. Wilder had messed around and choked on a fish bone in his back kitchen. His son, Raymond "Raybone" Wilder, Jr., was staying with him again—he and his daddy had "an understanding," you see—and Raybone was so stressed out that he ran over to Aunt Malaika's house instead of calling Ms. B., or Ms. Perez, or anybody, like he knew he should.

I don't know why he did this. When I think about it, it don't make no sense. He knew Aunt Malaika never liked him. Whenever she'd see him, she'd screw up her face, jaws sagging, and say, "A thirty-five-year-old man too grown to be sitting up in his daddy's house not working," but then she'd catch Mr. Wilder, Sr., huffing down the street again, his arms filled with a grease-stained paper bag full of whatever he'd scraped up from the church kitchen, and she'd just suck her teeth and stomp back into her dusty old house.

And even her house was hateful. The high porch steps sagged and sunk like they were ready to trip any fool crazy enough to want to walk up them. The back door didn't hardly stay shut if you closed it, and that front door would mangle any key in its lock. Most days she kept her door open. No need to lock it. Nobody was desperate enough to steal from Aunt Malaika.

Later, when they asked Raybone why he didn't just call 911 from his own home, he said his daddy's phone had got cut off and they ain't got no more minutes on their cell. I don't know about all that, but I do know that when he woke Aunt Malaika up, beating on the door like he crazy, she cussed him out and then charged him twenty-five cents for the phone call. Said that Raybone was as shiftless as his daddy, "didn't never work but always sitting somewhere, eating." Said his daddy was too big and greasy to be eating all that chicken and fried fish, anyway.

And when Raybone said, "But Ms. Laika, if you don't let me make this call, he gone be dead," Aunt Malaika started stuttering and sputtering so, that she snatched back the phone and slammed the door in poor Raybone's face.

The ambulance came right away when Mr. Wilder died—as soon as they got the call . . . a good fifteen minutes later. Raybone had broke his ankle running down her evil porch steps—his big old size fifteens fell right through the floor—and he had to limp down to Mr. Denton's place to make the call. But when Aunt Malaika hit the ground on 875 Randle, on the hottest day in July, she might as well have been laying dead in the street, because by the time that ambulance come, Aunt Malaika was long gone.

Reverend Preacher say in his sermon that Mrs. Malaika Hamilton had been a fine, upstanding woman, steadfast in the church and didn't nobody sitting on those hard mourner's pews dare say a contrary word.

Aunt Malaika never missed a meeting of the usher board, and her white gloves and uniform were always pristine (a fine feat, given the dust she let accumulate in the house she'd been living in). Aunt Malaika had been a member of the church longer than even the oldest deacon, and she had the dirt on damn near everyone. Still, she never would tell a soul, or at least I don't think she would. Not many saint points in that. To Aunt Malaika, gossip was a sin. Even so, that didn't stop her from staring you down with that old knowing look in her eye that let you know that she know that you know that she could tell if she wanted to tell, and you know if you keep on backsliding, you know someday she would.

So when Reverend Preacher peered under his glasses, meeting the gaze of every one of us, we didn't do nothing but listen. "Mrs. Hamilton," Reverend Preacher say, revving up. "I said, Mrs. Ma-la-i-ka Hamilton . . ."

"Yes," we replied in unison.

"You know you had to get it right," Reverend Preacher say, laughing. "Sister Hamilton didn't tolerate you de-se-crat-ing her name. Sister Hamilton was a fine example to you younger folk on how to live in the fullness of the Word."

"Yes."

"I say, *the fullness*."

"Yes, Lord."

"And Mrs. Hamilton was born and raised in the *Church*," he said, clutching his Bible, "part of that noble congregation called *Old School*."

We raised our heads and said, "Amen," praying he would soon hush up as the ushers scurried in their white padded shoes.

The doors of the church were open, but who would have thought that Aunt Malaika's soul didn't float through them.

It was true that Aunt Malaika's "steadfastness" had made her a hard woman to live with. At one point or another, everybody in the church had had some narrow dealing with her. Still, I was a little hurt, though not exactly surprised, when I got her call. Whatever happened, I never expected to see Aunt Malaika in Hell.

I don't know what I was expecting, but Hell is really small. I can hardly get my hips up in here. Despite all the fire and brimstone—you know how they say we like the heat—you can tell that Hell wasn't made for no black folk. The hallways are too narrow, and the ceiling is much too low. It keeps pressing down every time you take a step. I nearly cracked my skull trying to make my way to Aunt Malaika's raggedy room.

And the woman at the front desk just as mean and nasty—had the nerve to cut her eyes at me, like I was going to steal something.

I walked down the hall, the sulphur so thick I knew I'd be smelling it in my sleep.

Aunt Malaika shares a room with two other old women. I know this must be Hell because Aunt Malaika didn't like to share much of anything without making you feel guilty about it.

But if anyone could make a soul feel more weary in Hell, that would be Aunt Malaika. When I come in, she's sitting up on the top bunk, her fingers knotted and working in her lap, staring out a dingy window that somebody tried to cheer up with a yellow, faded crazy quilt. The stitches are all ragged and crooked, like somebody blind and shook with seizures sewed them. I can hardly see the pattern. I want to clear my throat, say hello, but it seems like I still can't speak in that woman's presence.

"Laika, baby, look like you got you some company."

Another old woman clutching a photo turns to stare at me. She wraps a tattered navy-blue sweater around her thin shoulders and smiles. Her teeth are blue and stained.

"Who is it? Can't be nobody I want to see," Aunt Malaika says. "Jimbo? Karen? Hollis?"

"No, it's me, Aunt Malaika." I nearly choke on the words, voice so quiet she can hardly hear me. I see her turn from the window and squint.

"Who the hell is 'me'?" she asks. "Ah, don't say nothing," she says before I can answer, recognition widening her eyes. "Got to be mealy-mouthed Mildred. You the only one that bother to keep my name straight."

I nearly fall back with the force of these words.

"What you bring me, girl, 'cause the food up in here ain't fit to feed a snake."

I hold out my palms, sweating.

She looks disgusted.

I could have kicked my own butt for coming empty-handed, but what a body supposed to bring a woman who swear she don't need anything? I'd been trying to figure out how to please this woman since before I was born, and from the frown on her face, I guess she was going to keep me trying now that she done worried herself into Hell.

She brushed back her braids and pulled a yellow cardigan over her ample breasts.

"Don't mind this," she said when she caught me staring. She tugged the *I'm Retired—What's Your Excuse?* T-shirt self-consciously. "It's too hot to be walking round here in all that mess. I don't know what made your cousin Hollis dress me in that awful, gaudy red dress. Knowing full well I wouldn't be caught out in no hussy slip like that."

"It was pink, not red," I said, "and I thought you looked nice, Aunt Lai . . . Malaika."

"You *would*," she said, narrowing her eyes at my flouncy sundress.

I was never her favorite niece.

She leaned forward, grabbing my wrist, and hissed in my ear.

"What you say, Aunt Malaika?" Her breath smelled like Juicy Fruit and Denture Klean.

"I *said*, don't you eat nothing up in here," she whispered loudly. "Don't eat a crumb or a cracker, and watch out for that heffa at the front desk. She sneaky. She'll mess around and have you singing a blues for every season."

"Okay, Aunt Malaika," I said slowly, like I understood. This heat and sulphur must have fried her poor brain.

"You best to listen to your grandmama," the plump one said. She was sitting in one of those green plastic deck chairs, her flowery duster spread out across her thick thighs. She'd been staring at a muted TV screen mounted in a corner of the wall. A skein of orange tangled yarn rested in her lap. I watched her pale gray eyes return to the black-and-white stories on the tube. The other one sat beside a faded chifforobe, the vanity table cluttered with warped and peeling photos of children, smiling and gap-toothed. They stared back at me, making me think of ice cream and pulpy lemonade, the kind the other "wayward" kids used to get when I was sweating in Sunday school.

"That your grandbaby?" she asked.

"I told you, she ain't," Aunt Malaika barked, gritting her teeth. "I ain't never had no children and ain't never wished I could."

I clasped my hand, nails biting into the palm flesh. Before I came, I said I was going to be nice to Aunt Malaika, like I always have, but she was testing me. Though nobody could ever say I wasn't grateful for how she took me in and raised me like her own, I never much cared for the way she had of not claiming me. No, I wasn't her natural born, but she was the closest thing to a mama I'd ever known. And if I wasn't her daughter, I might as well be, because all the other kids was scared of her and wouldn't have nothing to do with her.

That's probably why Hollis buried her in that red dress.

I decided to change the subject.

"So how you settling in, Aunt Malaika?"

"Well, what you think?" She looked at me like I had lost my mind. "One minute I'm minding my business, watering my rosebush—you know how they get during the summer—and the next, I'm trying to raise my head to meet my Maker. I look up and find myself in this Hellhole, and ain't a real rosebush here or even a drop of air-conditioning."

I look at her in disbelief.

"That's why I ain't never wanted no public assistance," she continued. "They'll welfare you right out of a good house and into the state penitentiary. It's too hot up in here, and I been trying to tell that old battle-ax up at the front desk, but she don't listen. Talking 'bout, 'Take it to Jesus . . .'"

"I'm so sorry," I say, and I'm starting to see what she means. I can hardly breathe myself, and I feel my sundress clinging to me, hot and sticky against my skin. "Why don't I open this window for you?" I ask, pulling back the curtain.

"It's *stuck*," she replied, rolling her eyes.

No, she never liked me, even though I was the only one who bothered to see about her. But I couldn't help myself. I wanted to fight it off, but here I was again, trying to prove my worthiness. I tugged harder on the windowpane, trying to force it up with the tips of my fingers. It didn't budge, but I did see a sight that made me still and queasy.

The window was nailed shut, big red rusting nails driven deep into the windowsill. Just beyond it in a freshly cut yard was a rosebush, so big and beautiful, perfectly rounded with its soft petals and luscious leaves gleaming like God's Great Own, like something straight out of Eden.

No wonder Aunt Malaika stayed glued to that window.

That's when I started wondering what Old Gray Eyes was missing in that TV, and Miss Thin—what kind of a sad story was hidden behind those children's gap-toothed smiles and eyes?

I kept staring at the rosebush until it moved. I thought it moved, or maybe that was just—

A thorny branch snakes up and hisses at me, then slams hard into the windowpane, cracking the glass. An odor begins to fill the room so foul and thick that Miss Thin starts to wail.

"Baby, just shut it," Aunt Malaika says, waving at the curtains. "Shut it quick before I have to listen to Velma all day." Her voice is tired, almost resigned. I have never heard Aunt Laika sound this way.

I yank back the tattered curtains, listening for the next assault, but the rosebush soon tires and slinks back into itself. The room is quiet, silence falls around us like a heavy shawl. Below the ragged calm of Miss Thin's breathing, I hear the low-voiced hum of distant climate control. Perhaps a heater.

Miss Thin slumps in her vanity chair, the pictures tumbling over in their gilded frames. Gray Eyes falls back into the rhythm of her voiceless stars, their movements a slow pantomime against the colorless screen.

I sit next to Aunt Malaika, my knee pressed against her thigh, and stare at the hidden window. Aunt Malaika loved her rosebush. She prized its roots more than any sour fruit on her swaybacked peach trees. Before the sun rose, she was out with her rusty watering can in hand. And three times each day, before it set, she would water it again, sprinkling it from her cupped hands as if it was her own back-porch baptism.

When I was a child, I used to watch her from my bedroom window. These quiet times, when dayclean was just bending into daydone, she chose to be alone. She never let me help her, afraid that I might pour too much or crush the delicate petals and leaves with my eager hands. But she let me watch, and for that I was grateful. Her rosebush was the only thing of beauty she allowed in her yard.

"Remember how you used to wipe my eyes with rose petals, after you bathed me and put me to bed?" I say suddenly. "Your rosebush had a special scent. I ain't smelled it in years, but look like I woke up the other day and heard you call my name."

"How you remember a thing like that?" she asks.

She gives me another look, not so long, not so knowing, then scratches her scalp, flicking dandruff from a white braid. For the first time, I imagine the young girl in her, what she must have looked like when she was close to my age. She still has that head of hair all the other usher mothers envied. I look around. I don't see any mirrors. I guess you don't need none in Hell. I wonder if she knows.

"When I was a youngun, not such a slip as you, but young enough," she begins, "them old mothers used to say a night-bath in rose water kept a girl's future soft and sweet. Something 'bout sealing a woman's ways."

I laugh. "That *is* sweet."

She grunts. "Oh, that ain't nothing but some hoodoo mess, them old ways from folk that don't know no better. You feeling mighty 'soft and sweet' now?"

I was, I want to say, *till you got ugly*.

"That your grandbaby?" Miss Thin asks again. It's like her mind is one of those old phonographs, and she's stuck on the same groove. She's fondling her framed pictures, smiling, spittle hanging from her lip.

Aunt Malaika frowns and shifts on the bed. "No, Velma, that's my daughter. How old you think I is, anyway?"

I don't say nothing, just look at Aunt Malaika.

"Well, what her name? You been sitting over there whispering and ain't introduced nobody."

"Her name Hollis—"

"—Mildred," I mutter.

"Mildred," she continues, not missing a beat, "has come to visit me, and we was talking, *minding our business*," she adds with emphasis. It occurs to me that Aunt Malaika is possessive of a visitor, even me. This is gratifying, and I can't hardly contain my smile, grinning ear to ear.

"Well, Mildred, welcome to Hell, child," Miss Thin says brightly. "I know it ain't what you thought it was, but we gon' do our best to make you enjoy your stay. You must have done something mighty bad, though, something sinful, to come down here, but I can't tell what it is, sweet as you seem to be. But you never know . . . they don't tell you nothing. Just sign you in and lock you up."

"Never know?" Gray Eyes snapped to attention, her head pivoting away from the TV screen. "What you mean you never know? What somebody got to tell you 'bout yourself that you don't already know? You here the same reason why we all here."

"And what's that?" Miss Thin says, her eyes darting round the room.

"'Cuz you triflin'. You was triflin' when you was living and now you triflin' in death."

"I *ain't* triflin'!" Miss Thin yells, banging her tiny fists on her gilded keepsake chest. "Is it wrong to want a little bit of loving for yourself? Is it wrong to want somebody just for you?"

"That's the problem. He wasn't for you. He was *married*, and all them children you doting on, sitting on that desk, ain't got no part of you in them. They his, and his alone." She paused, doubled back. "Naw, that ain't right. They his—*and his wife's*."

"It ain't true," Miss Thin says, her eyes pleading with me. I knot the hem of my dress, fingers working, nervous—same thing I did when I was a child. I don't want to hear this. In fact, I want to go.

"And if you had the backbone enough to love a married man, you should have had backbone enough to love your ownself!"

"Stop it, Gladys," Aunt Malaika says. "That's enough from you."

"Yeah," Miss Thin says, between sobs. "We not gon' talk about why you here, now, are we?"

"No, we're not," Aunt Malaika says severely. "Seem like you two would get tired of fussing and fighting. Ain't none of us going nowhere."

"Well, at least we have this nice young thing to keep us company," Miss Thin says, perking up.

Aunt Malaika look like she want to whoop her.

"Velma, she ain't here to stay. She just visiting, and in fact, she 'bout to go," she says, struggling to stand up. Baffled, I hold her by the elbow and let her lean on my shoulder as she gets to her feet. She's reaching a bare toe across the floor, looking for her slippers, fuzzy teddy bears she never would have worn in life. "Come on, child," she adds, hurried. "Wouldn't want you to miss your bus."

"But Aunt Malaika, I just got here, and we ain't hardly talked," I say, as she dusts me off and straightens my loose shoulder strap. Suddenly, I feel like the floor been swept from underneath me. Why she rushing me out now?

"Mildred, we done said all we need to say. You look good, so I guess, hard as it was, I done good," she says, brushing her hard knuckles against my cheek. She looks at me with something I've never seen from her before: satisfaction. "You always was a good child, but so scared of stepping on your own shadow, I couldn't hardly get you to stand on your own feet." She stares up into my face, searching. "But you standing now, ain't you? And now you must go. Visiting hours should be just about up."

"You ain't got to go home . . ." Miss Thin says, shaking her head.

"Well, if you don't want her to stay, you better get her out of here," Gladys says, cutting her off. "'Cause when that heffa come with those pills . . ."

Aunt Malaika sighs. "I know." She turns to me. "Come on, Mildred, give your mama a kiss."

I look at her, feeling both guilt and relief. I move quickly to the door, before her mood changes—or she changes her mind. I'm her daughter. That's what she said. No turning back from that. She's satisfied.

"Should I come back, some time next week? Next Sunday?"

She pats a loose braid and places it smoothly behind her ear. Her fingers have a marked tremor. We have the exact same ears, shaped like little rose petals. Why didn't I notice that before?

She looks troubled. "Baby, if you like. But you got to go now. And Mildred . . ."

"Yes?" I say, standing at the door.

She reaches out, and for a moment I think she will hug me, but she grasps my wrists. Her hands are cold—deadly cold. "Don't look behind you," she says, staring at me until I understand. "Remember."

Forget what they tell you. Hell is very small, and crowded. The ceilings are low and the hallways are narrow. A full-bodied soul like me can't hardly make no elbow room. And the air, the air smells like pot liquor and cooking grease, like something holed up in a smoky kitchen.

I am holding my breath as I hurry through the winding corridors, the ceiling getting lower and lower, like some kind of strange limbo. Eyes averted, my hands resting at my sides, I am not holding back tears. I am not thinking of my Aunt Malaika sitting on her bunk bed by a wavering window, staring at a strip of green, receding. I am not concentrating on white roses, sharp elbows resting in a dusty windowsill. As I finally pass through the gates, I am not thinking of my mother, and I don't look back, no, not never again.

Blues for Sister Rose

by Michael A. Gonzales

E ddie Taylor began toughening his heart shortly after departing the dusty Atlanta railroad station. From the moment he stepped aboard the colored-only car of the train dressed in a dapper dark-blue summer suit, crisp white shirt, and two-toned shoes like the ones Miles Davis styled in the latest *Down Beat*, Eddie promised himself not to be overwhelmed by the majestic metropolis of Manhattan. A sax player since he was a teenager, Eddie prayed he had enough musical moxie to survive in the chocolate city of ambition known as Harlem.

"Just be cool," he mumbled to himself, a mantra that had become the slogan of his new life since returning from overseas in December 1953. Luckily, his old Korean War buddy Ronald Mallory had offered him a place to stay and the possibility of a few club gigs.

One of those light-skinned, pretty motherfuckers who loved the sound of his own voice, Ronald had thrilled Eddie with Negro Heaven stories about sizzling Harlem nightclubs, foxy mamas strutting down One Hundred Twenty-fifth, and simmering plates of chicken and waffles from Wells'. Lying in their bunks as planes roared across the night sky, Ronald mumbled, "You know, with your bebop ways on that there trumpet, jazzbos will be treating you like a black prince. Forget about Charlie Parker, 'cause folks will be screaming your name."

"Man, don't disrespect Bird," Eddie replied solemnly. "That man is more than a genius, he's a saint."

"No disrespect meant," Ronald answered. "I'm just saying, with your talent on the sax, Mr. Parker might have to move over a little to make room for your country butt."

For the entire eight hundred fifty miles, Eddie was as excited as a small boy in Santa's lap, imagining that this up-North paradise would be akin to the jazzy Betty Boop cartoons he had enjoyed as a child: an animated world of voluptuous vixens, blazing bebop bands and zooming Cadillacs under a low-hanging sky. Believing he would soon be reborn in the spirit of soaring skyscrapers and scorching jazz, Eddie Taylor was ready for his solo.

After pushing through anxious crowds at Penn Station the following afternoon, Eddie and Ronald sped up Sixth Avenue in the crimson 1954 Buick Roadmaster convertible. Enthralled by the din of bustling crowds, screaming neon, and rowdy construction workers, Eddie almost cried.

Looking at Ronald's freshly conked tresses, custom-tailored threads, and fine automobile with its tacky red and black interior, Eddie thought his boy looked like he had just tap-danced out of the glossy pages of *Esquire*. "Where did you get the bread for such a fine ride, Ronald?"

"First thing, nobody calls me by that lame name anymore," Ronald answered. "Uptown folks call me Cozy."

"Cozy?"

"Yeah, 'cause I can get whatever makes them feel comfortable. Being a bartender in Harlem, I gots to make sure folks are taken care of right. Or, in my case, I make sure they're cozy."

"So you make sure things are right. I get it. So, Cozy, where you find such a beautiful car?"

"My boss owns a couple of bars uptown. He loans me this piece on a steady so I can make my runs."

With his luggage safely stashed in the cluttered trunk of the car, Eddie sat in the plush passenger seat like a dark-faced Columbus joyfully absorbing the New World. Charlie Parker's superb "East of the Sun (and West of the Moon)" blared from the car's mono radio. Eddie couldn't have thought of a better soundtrack.

"You all right there, Eddie?" Cozy asked, playfully smacking his friend on the leg. Too vain to wear glasses, he often looked as though light shone in his eyes. Smoking filterless Camels, Cozy wiped cigarette ashes from his otherwise spotless shirt.

Startled by the sting of Cozy's slap, Eddie felt like a drowning man coming up for air. "I'm cool," he said. "Just trying to take it all in."

"Boy, you could live in this city a hundred years and never take it all in."

Making a sharp right at Seventy-second Street, Cozy blazed the bulky ride to Central Park West before making a sharp left at the corner. Marveling at the elegant apartment houses on the left and lush park on the right, Eddie gripped the bottom of his seat.

With a beaming smile, Cozy looked at Eddie's frightened face and chuckled. "Don't worry, I ain't about to let nothing happen to this beautiful ride."

"It's not the car I'm worried about," Eddie gulped.

"Don't worry, I'm not about to let anything happen to *you* either."

Crossing an invisible border at One Hundred Tenth, the white-lettered street signs read Eighth Avenue as the stately glamour of luxury apartment buildings were soon replaced by sagging tenements and brown-faced children splashing beneath the cold water of an open fire hydrant. Meaty-armed mamas leaned out of open windows while pretty Catholic school girls clad in penny loafers, white socks, and long plaid skirts sloughed against a lamppost watching corner boys shoot dice against a wall. A few feet away a decrepit shoeshine man polished a fancy player's shoes and a dirty-faced boy hawked copies of the colored newspaper, the *Lenox Observer*.

Only a blind man wouldn't have realized they were finally in Harlem.

Pulling in front of Obie's, a sweet-smelling greasy spoon on One Hundred Thirty-fifth, sharp-dressed Cozy double-parked. Unpleasantly reminded that it had been hours since his last meal, Eddie took a deep breath and reveled in the aroma of hamburgers, scrambled eggs, and freshly brewed coffee wafting from the dingy diner's open door. Unlocking the car door, his stomach rumbled.

"After we get you settled, I'll go get a few burgers," Cozy laughed, hauling the oversized suitcase and saxophone case from the trunk. Placing the baggage on the curb, he pointed at a beautiful brownstone two doors down from the diner. "All right, private, forward march!"

Following Cozy through the front door, Eddie walked into the brownstone's enchanting foyer. Gazing at the high ceilings and polished parquet floors, Eddie put down his heavy bags on the earth-toned rug. "Jesus," he mumbled, gazing at the stained-glass windows above the door and the fresh-cut roses in the Tiffany crystal vase on the hallway table. "This castle is a far cry from the tenement you told me about when we were in the Army."

"Before you start thinking I'm loaded, this is my Aunt Dolly's place. She's up at the Vineyard for the summer." Using a pseudo-snooty voice, Cozy held his thumb and pinkie as though he was lifting a fragile china cup. "More than likely having high tea with Dorothy West and the rest of the Sepia Sisterhood as we speak."

"Damn Aunt Dolly!" Eddie screamed with country boy awe.

"She owns Unity Funeral Home over on Eighth Avenue. Living Negroes can make a pretty penny burying dead ones. The best part about staying here is, you don't have to find a real job until after Labor Day. All you gots to do is blow that damn horn and keep the house neat. Anyway, enough with all that."

"What about a job?" Eddie asked.

"My boss man says he'll be able to get you a temporary cabaret card. But for now, you can go upstairs and get settled. Your room will be at the top of the stairs, to the right. Try to get a nap, 'cause tonight we gonna be stepping out."

"Stepping out?"

"Look, what kind of friend would I be if I let your first night in the Apple be spent watching *The Jackie Gleason Show*? You're going with me into Wonderland. Another thing, polish that horn, 'cause she's coming with us."

Decorated in girly wallpaper, an antique dresser drawer, and a paisley throw rug at the bottom of the queen-size bed, the guest room looked to Eddie like an oversized dollhouse. Peering out of the window, he was thrilled by the sparkling sunshine spraying warm rays over tarred rooftops and the colossal water towers in the distance.

There was a handcrafted night table next to the bed that had copies of *Jet*, *Hue*, and the latest *Lenox Observer*. Though the room was quiet, the tabloid type screamed: QUEER MENACE! BY TERRELL THOMAS. Eddie wasn't quite sure what the bold words meant, but after three years of fighting Commies, he'd had enough with menaces of any kind.

Bending down, he snapped open the saxophone case, pulled out the gleaming Buescher Aristocrat alto sax, and caressed the brass as though it were the supple breast of a beautiful woman.

"If you don't live it, it won't come out your horn," Charlie Parker once said. Sticking the mouthpiece between his lips, Eddie blew a frantic improvisation that echoed the chaos of the city. Afterwards, sliding the sax underneath the bed, Eddie stripped his suit and hung all of his clothes in the closet. Minutes later, curled up on the bed, his snores were as loud as the train he had rode in on.

Two years before Uncle Sam had snatched Eddie's skinny ass out of the briar patches of Buckhead, his two best pals in the world were neighbors and classmates Linwood Mosby and Calvin Freeman. Known amongst the locals as the Three Musketeers, they had been best friends since the days of short pants and Sunday school.

Bigheaded Calvin was a large, somewhat slow teenager with bulging muscles and a gentle temperament. Even so, that didn't stop the sheriff's crazy boy from beating Calvin to death one rainy autumn as God peeped down from beyond the clouds. Supposedly Calvin had raped a young white girl with his stare and the sheriff's son just couldn't stand a "reckless eye-balling nigger."

Hearing of his friend's death the following morning, Eddie's heart was coated with a thin film of ice. Mentally sliding into another world, he escaped the pain of his friend's murder (how he wished local colored folks would stop saying "the boy is in a better place") through the ecstasy of jazz. Twirling the radio dial late one night, Eddie tuned in to a static-filled station that introduced the brooding teenager to the suffering and sadness of Coleman Hawkins, John Coltrane, Dexter Gordon, and, most importantly, Charlie Parker.

Days later, after dusting off his daddy's ancient saxophone buried in the basement, Eddie got his old man to show him the basics. His father had once jammed in Dixieland bands before getting married and settling down. Pops was surprised how quickly the boy caught on. Eddie might not have been a prodigy, but he wasn't no joke either.

Baptized by the harmonic spirits that washed over him, Eddie Taylor's new religion was jazz. When the inevitable call came to serve his country, the first thing Eddie packed was his horn, hoping they would put him in the band instead of on the battlefield.

Returning from Korea three years later, Eddie's father noticed that his boy was doing a lot of tight-lipped moping. "If you gots a problem, boy, you needs to spit it out," his father demanded.

"I don't know, Pop, much as I love you and Ma, coming back to the South was the last thing I really wanted to do. I'm scared if I stay here too long I might have some white man's blood staining my hands."

"You still thinking about that Calvin boy, huh?"

"Don't you?"

"Of course I do, Eddie, but where you want to go to escape? Chicago, Detroit, one of them cold cities where the hawk flies low?"

"Better a low-flying hawk than that high-flying Jim Crow. Naw, forget about the Midwest, I'm bound for Harlem."

"Is that a new song you wrote?"

"No, it's a state of mind."

"Hell, an old horn blower like myself can understand that," his father laughed. "But you know, boy, there's prejudice in Harlem too."

"Of course," Eddie replied. "But at least it's not the kind where they drag you from your home in the middle of the night and no one ever sees you alive again. Riding back home this afternoon I saw a chain gang on the side of the road and I started feeling like this entire state is a jail cell. I don't want to be locked up, I want to be a jazz musician."

"So you think you going to Harlem and change the world with your horn?"

"I ain't saying all that," Eddie smiled, hugging his dad, "but I can damn well try."

The joyful noise of New York City children woke Eddie from a deep sleep. Startled by banshee screams as the kids played freeze tag, ring-a-levio, hopscotch, or some other ghetto game, Eddie stretched the knots and kinks out of his lanky frame. He walked over to the curtained window clad in striped boxer shorts and a white T-shirt, and watched as the descending sun colored the heavens with its fiery glow. Knocking hard on the thick oak door, Cozy bounced into the room wearing a Dobbs hat and stylish suit.

"You still sleep, Country?"

"Naw, just got up."

"Good, 'cause you can sleep when you're dead. This night, it's all about living." Glancing at the sleek watch on his left wrist, he added, "It's almost eight, and I got a dynamite night planned for your coming-out party." Across the room, Eddie laughed. "What's so funny?"

"Nothing, just nervous laughter, I guess."

Pulling a smoke from the jacket of his Priestley suit, Cozy lit up. "Yeah, well, why don't you nervously get your ass into some clothes so we can get on down the Great Black Way? We're going to dinner at Frazier's Dining Room at nine o'clock."

"Whose dining room?"

"Frazier's. They got the best damn chicken and dumplings on planet Harlem. My little cousin Bootsie is a waitress over there, so she doesn't always put everything on the tab."

Opening the creaky closet door, Eddie pulled out a pressed black seersucker suit. "Should I still bring my horn?"

"Ain't that why you came to the jungle, to play for the natives? Seriously, I'm taking you over to meet this friend named Nicole Rose. Folks sometimes call her Sister Rose. She's a hot young singer, a blues-crooning jazz girl with a small combo. Been around Harlem for a minute doing her thing. Her sax player got his call from Uncle Sam, so she needs a replacement fast."

Smiling broadly, Eddie screamed, "You serious, Ronald?"

"As a heart attack, Jack. And let this be the last time I tell you, that Ronald shit went out of style with top hats and tails. Folks in Harlem just call me Cozy, or nothing at all."

☙

After midnight, parking on the corner of St. Nick and One Hundred Forty-seventh, Cozy snatched the saxophone case from the backseat and handed it to Eddie. Already buzzed from the booze at dinner and later at Small's Paradise, slurring Cozy said, "We're just in time for the first performance." Stumbling from the car, each slammed his door shut.

Standing in front of Macero's Deli across the street, a small posse of ragged teenagers puffed reefer and harassed passing pedestrians as though they owned the bustling block. Dressed identically in faded denim jackets, tight jeans, and threadbare sneakers, the rowdy delinquents couldn't have cared less that their ruckus was keeping awake decent folks.

One dangerous-looking boy with a freckled face, dirty red hair, and a black cloud floating over his head had obviously watched too many Bogart pictures and thought of himself as a tough guy. Standing beneath the streetlight, he grimaced at Eddie, revealing a tainted gold tooth.

"Don't look at them crazy kids," Cozy warned. "They're members of a street gang, the Amsterdam Angels. Them boys ain't nothing but trouble with a capital T." As though on cue, one of the punks tossed a Coke bottle and it smashed in the middle of the street. "The one with the gold tooth is Red Jackson, their fearless leader. Let's get over to the joint before one of them suckers makes me lose my religion."

Walking the two blocks to the after-hours spot, Cozy stopped a few paces from the downward staircase. Touching Eddie gently on the arm, he said, "You know, I haven't been completely honest with you about this bar. I don't want you to go in there and lose your mind or anything."

"Why would I?"

"Well, it's a different kind of scene down here. I thought I should warn you first."

"You're confusing me."

"All right," Cozy finally blurted. "This place is a gay bar."

"A happy bar?"

Despite his seriousness, Cozy laughed. "Not happy, you country bumpkin, homosexuals. As in freaks, queers, fags, bull dykes. The bar's name might say Jazzy's Jumpers outside, but all the regulars just call it The Secret."

"The Secret?"

"Yeah, as in not wanting other people to know your business."

"Do you have any secrets, Cozy?"

Sheepishly, he glanced at his old friend. "Look, I love pussy as much as the next man, but every now and then, you know . . ."

For a minute, Eddie was stunned. He had heard about stuff like that, but in Georgia those "funny" things were never discussed. Eddie slowly exhaled. "You don't have to explain, it's all right. You're still my friend and all, just don't be trying none of that 'secret' stuff with me."

Touched by Eddie's humor and understanding, Cozy smiled. "Come on, let's go inside."

Tucked in the basement of a cheap hotel at 6 St. Nicholas Place, away from the prying peepers of a judgmental public, the small bar was a place where one could be free. In addition to the regulars, a fair number of straight writers, painters, and poets also hung out in the crowed room. A stunning Aaron Douglas painting of Savoy dancers hung over the bar.

Occasionally a few of the bleary-eyed Amsterdam Angels hassled customers outside ("Hey fairies, where yo wings at?"), but they generally kept their knuckleheaded abuse on a verbal level. Recently, as the latest headlines indicated, the crusading colored folks from the *Lenox Observer* had thrown gasoline on the fire with their bristling series of articles aimed at ridding Harlem of "degenerate homosexuals."

While most of The Secret's neighbors knew of the club's existence (wagging their tongues from paint-chipped windows, exchanging sharp glances from the beat-up stoops), the sordid stories of homosexual pedophilia and anti-Christian ways had encouraged folks to be fearful and resentful. The Secret was forced to pose as a "private club" for the sake of the pesky vice squad, and they sold mimeographed membership cards at the door for a quarter. Inside the bar, a sensuous transvestite barmaid named Sable, whose fluttering movements called to mind a high-strung ostrich, mixed drinks with the artistic skill of a barroom Bearden.

The plate-glass window was painted black and multicolored Christmas lights were strung up behind the bar. The joint stank of cigarette smoke, fried chicken wings and disinfectant. The brown linoleum floor was sticky from spilled drinks and old chewing gum. Awaiting the singer's entrance, Nicole's musical quartet of saxophone, bass, drums, and piano warmed up the audience with a heated version of Billy Strayhorn's "Lush Life."

Finally strutting to the center of the bandstand, Nicole stood silent for a moment. Staring into the blissfully intoxicated faces of The Secret's regular patrons, she noticed Chip, a dark-skinned writer with a vicious appetite for strong gin and strange men; red-boned Tyrone, who bummed cigarettes while claiming to be saving his cents for a sex change; mannish Helen and femme Alice, who often posed as "cousins" in the eyes of the outside world.

With a sweltering voice that was sensual as a French kiss, Nicole was clad in a black evening gown. A full-figured light-skinned woman, she was thirty-five years young. Wearing her trademarked rose pinned between heavy cleavage and red satin mules with six-inch heels, Nicole's bone-straight hair glimmered under the white lights.

A singer since she first belted in the choir of White Rock Baptist Church in the backwater town of Troy, Ohio, at the age of seven, Nicole Rose possessed a radiant passion reflected in her hypnotic voice. A biracial girl who had never known her Italian daddy, Nicole was like Dinah Washington without the amphetamine attitude, Billie Holiday without the heroin visage and Lena Horne without the fame. Sharing the highball and ashtray–cluttered table near the stage with the singer's girlfriend Michelle, who wore a red boa and a short skirt revealing luscious legs, Eddie was happy.

"Our lady of perpetual suffering," snapped a drunken queen. "Girl, don't you know you too young to be so real?

Mixing her own brew of bleak romanticism into the lyrics, Nicole roared through earthy covers of "September in the Rain," "Good Morning Heartache," and "Harlem on My Mind." Still, the true heart-stopper of her set began when Nicole groaned the self-penned blues of "Nothing Lasts Forever." Opening the number with a sad and spooky piano solo, Nicole's song detailed the misadventures of, "A lowlife gal in high-heeled shoes / She'll step on your heart and give you the blues / but still she loves you, yes she loves you . . ."

Listening intensely, Eddie drifted on a sorrowful sea where Nicole's stormy voice blew like a dangerous wind. As the drummer pounded a beat that resembled running feet and the shrill sax sounded like a nightingale's mating call, Eddie was tempted to rush the stage with his own alto. But when the deep bass dragged the gasping audience further into a rhythmic abyss, he thought it best to be properly introduced.

Frozen in their seats, the spectators took a moment to warm up after the brittle chill Nicole's voice had sent through their bloodstreams. The gnawing in their bellies felt like starving tenement rats. Then, after the last frigid jaw had dropped, the gloomy room of crimson decadence exploded with mad applause. It was as though the sky had split and thunder cracked the fragile heavens.

More charged than an electric wire, the cheering crowd threw money onto the small stage. "We adore you!" screamed a manic queen over the noise.

Flipping her shoulder-length hair with the flair of a damaged diva, Nicole joked, "Well, I'm glad you motherfuckers know class when you hear it. Thank you." Taking a bow, she stepped regally from the stage. She was like an uptown goddess who had just performed a miracle, and her followers longed to touch her.

"You were wonderful, baby!" Michelle swooned. Hugging her blue-voiced girl, she added, "I don't think you've ever sounded better." They had met eleven months past when Michelle first arrived from the Jamaican parish of Spanish Town and was waiting tables at a popular West Indian restaurant called Dakota's Hot Pot.

"Thank you," said Nicole, kissing Michelle's painted lips tenderly. "But don't hold me so tight, baby doll. Save some for later."

Batting her long eyelashes, Nicole lit a Winston and slowly exhaled. Like most urban blues mamas who had growled in too many dives for too many fools for too little money, Nicole had developed a rather sardonic worldview, but Michelle had a special way of easing those pains. And when it came to her passion for Michelle, she had no shame.

Eddie stared as Nicole and Michelle performed their romantic mating dance. Naïve, he didn't quite understand everything that had been rapidly thrown his way. Men with men, women with women, it was all a little confusing. He stood and bowed as though being introduced to royalty, then kissed Nicole's bejeweled hand. "Sister Rose, I presume," he said, working that Georgia charm.

"You must be the horn player I've been hearing about," she answered with grace.

Straight to the point, Eddie blurted, "I have my horn. Would you like me to play for you?"

Digging his country boy ways, Nicole took to him immediately. "Baby, if Cozy here says you can jam, I'll just take his word for it. He ain't known for steering people wrong." Rummaging through her purse, she found an eyebrow pencil and a makeup-stained napkin. She scribbled her Lenox Terrace address and phone number, then handed it to Eddie. "You just meet me at my apartment tomorrow at six o'clock, and everything will be copasetic."

By the following evening, Eddie had been hired to tour the Harlem chitlin circuit with the fleshy uptown Venus. While it had been his desire to be one of those angry avant-garde beboppers fighting a war against the tired traditionalists, Eddie figured playing the blues with Nicole beat a blank.

It wasn't a bad set-up though, Eddie thought, as Nicole Rose and her gutbucket sidemen crisscrossed through the streets of the pulsating black metropolis: from Saturday-night rent parties to Sunday-afternoon weddings, from Friday-night fish fries to Saturday-evening birthday parties. Then, much later in the debauched night, the entire drunken combo trekked to The Secret and musically soared for pocket change and loose dollars.

If Nicole was feeling especially generous after a night of wailing and raving, she'd invite a few scattered souls to her ornate apartment—with its gaudy crystal chandelier, Eames living room set and bone carpet—and cook some country eggs and bacon while the piano man played Jelly Roll jams on the shiny black Baldwin grand. Only in Harlem for two weeks, and Eddie was already beginning to feel at home.

Two months later, the entire group gathered at Nicole's crib after a

Minton's gig. Gulping freshly squeezed orange juice while awaiting their host's special announcement, the group fell quiet when Nicole clanged her crystal glass with a fork.

"I want to make a toast to our special guest, Mr. Willy Harris." Tilting her glass toward the only stranger in the room, she added, "Mr. Harris, who is offering us the first contract to his recently formed record label."

Grabbing the stylishly attired Willy Harris, an impish colored fellow who was the co-owner of Checkerboard Records, she kissed him moistly on the cheek. Willy, chewing on an unlit Cuban dressed in his trademarked plaid jacket and matching bow tie, smiled uncomfortably.

From where Eddie stood, it was obvious that Willy hated to be kissed, especially by a woman. "After years of looking for rainbows in trash heaps, I finally found a label willing to take a chance on my black ass," she said, laughing. Looking like a wounded puppy, Michelle stood silently in the corner and smiled.

Having signed Nicole Rose to record her debut disc, Willy wanted to get her behind the mic the following day. With Checkerboard Studios finally built, the musical arrangements complete, Willy planned on producing the sessions himself. After hiring the orchestra to sweeten her gritty blues sound, there was no money left in the kitty for practice sessions, but Willy was sure Nicole and her band were seasoned enough to read the charts he had prepared, copying Nelson Riddle's style. His sole musical vision was to slowly ease Nicole Rose from the blues sty where she was so content and transform her into the latest pop sensation.

"She'll be perfect, like Negress Sinatra," Harris had bragged to his partner. "Blues singers get treated like prize pigs. Everybody loves them, but they're still regulated to the mud." His smile beamed, his fingers snapped. Still, he realized it was more than Nicole's sound he would have to soften. He knew from his own experience that odd enigmas which couldn't be easily defined were usually rejected. Nicole would just have to understand that her "weakness" for women would have to stay permanently on the back burner. For public relations purposes, Willy thought as he glanced toward the hussy heathen who was Nicole's woman, Checkerboard would have to find their only artist a "boyfriend": a handsome young man that their future star could pose next to in newsreels and chat about in fan magazines.

Certainly, Nicole Rose would have to reform her wicked ways, Willy thought. Whoever heard of a pussy-eating female singing on *The Ed Sullivan Show*? Of course, he reasoned, if she wanted a career bad enough, Nicole would just have to learn a thing or two about decency.

Hearing church bells toll over the ecstatic voices in Nicole's apartment that Sunday morning, Willy Harris mumbled, "Amen."

That same morning, the gritty streets of Harlem were blistering from an oppressive heat wave as sweaty Sunday church folks ambled to the Lord's house for services.

Ten blocks north and three steps down from Nicole Rose's apartment, a fiery storefront preacher with a shock of wild gray hair and a loose-fitting black suit eagerly anticipated the full effect that his sermon would have on his brood of holy rollers.

Inspired by the glory he felt when hearing of the powerful sermons of Adam Clayton Powell, Jr., over at Abyssinian Baptist, the portly Reverend Dixon decided to sow the seeds of his own dark crusade, namely ridding Harlem of the countless "homo freaks and lezzies." Hell, Dixon had even invited his friend Terrell Thomas, the popular columnist from the *Lenox Observer* who had gotten the ball rolling.

It was rumored that most of Reverend Dixon's copy was scribbled in various sugar shacks as he guzzled Scotch on Saturday night, but by Sunday morn his words were sober. Shabbily dressed in a slept-in suit, Thomas stood in the rear of the church and watched as the minister strode to the altar.

Standing in front of the congregation, leather-bound Bible in hand, Reverend Dixon waited until the last tambourine rattled before leading his faithful flock toward the brimstone wrath of Judgment Day. Weeping crocodile tears, the old-time minister of Holy Ghost Pentecostal Ministries began his sermon.

"Oh-o-oh sinner, where will you stand . . . when Heaven begins raining fire and the Lord puts out his hand?"

Dusty ceiling fans blew hot air into solemn faces while Reverend Dixon's booming voice graphically detailed the blazing hoofs of hastening horses, the apocalyptic wail of Gabriel's gleaming trumpet over the honeyed voices of white-winged angels and the juicy fruits of paradise that awaited God's unwavering servants.

Streams of sweat trickled down Dixon's surly face as he denunciated the "degenerate homosexuals" who were degrading the streets of Harlem. Carefully avoiding eye contact with the choir director, whom everyone suspected had more sugar in his blood than most people put on their cereal, Reverend Dixon confidently bellowed: "Harlem society is full of queers. Unnatural folks, dear Jesus, destined for damnation in the infernos of Hell. Creeping . . . I said, creeping in the shadows like rodents. They creep and they sneak, though Jesus sees. They can't hide from you, Lord. Yes, the queer menace creeps amongst us. These evil, carefree creatures influence our children, luring them into the Devil's inferno. They ruin our community with their vile ways, but these freaks will not go unnoticed, because God sees all!"

Wiping his atheist brow with a stained handkerchief, the reporter was amused by the congregation. As the combustion of their beliefs surged though their bodies, they stirred in their seats, suddenly possessed by sanctified spirits.

"Save them, Jesus!" shouted a recent convert, a former party girl who now bathed in the blood of her savior, washing away her shame with holy water. "It's an abomination, Jesus. Abomination!"

As the voices grew louder and their movements more intense, Terrell sneakily gulped from the small bottle of White Label he had stashed in his suit pocket.

The newly opened offices and studios of Checkerboard Records were located on the fifth floor of an old warehouse on Riverside Drive and One Hundred Thirty-second Street in a building that was formerly a printing plant specializing in raunchy dime-store pulp novels, nudist-colony stag magazines and personalized church calendars. The massive loft still had a tinge of turpentine misting in the air.

Returning to the studio after the album cover shoot with photographer Bert Andrews, Willy exited the elevator. In the beige deco-designed waiting room, the walls were covered with framed eight-by-ten black-and-whites of Willy Harris posing with old-school jitterbugs Cab Calloway and Count Basie, candy-voiced dames Ruth Brown and Ella Fitzgerald, and assorted others.

Walking by the secretary's desk through yet another door, Willy passed the drab administrative offices where his cranky business partner, Monroe Levy, spent most of his day pacing the floor, complaining about cashflow.

If music was Willy Harris's god, then the studio was his temple. From the time he was a little boy, music had flowed through his soul. Making the rounds with his janitor father, whose job it was to sweep, mop, and polish the offices of various Tin Pan Alley music publishers downtown, Lil' Willy, as his pops still called him, caught the boogie-woogie fever young. Trekking from their uptown tenement to those glossy downtown sound factories became the equivalent of a divine revelation, like seeing God's face in one's dreams. Without saying a word, this little black boy had observed the birth of musical creations from the moment they were crumbs of an idea to the printing of the sheet music (which grumpy men like Monroe Levy's own daddy were hired to hawk) to its eventual recording by one of the popular big bands.

Willy Harris's skull buzzed with three-minute pop symphonies, those Technicolor luxuriant champagne soundtracks where violins quivered, piano strings shivered, flutes were fluent in romance languages and a horn section was cooler than a polar bear; with the music meticulously arranged and elegantly dreamy, this was to be the sound of Sister Rose's album *Nothing Lasts Forever.*

Puffing on a cigarette an hour after the photo shoot, Nicole Rose was stressed. It had always been easy to play the role of the bitchy ice princess, but inside she was shattered. Standing outside in a floral dress and matching brocade-heeled shoes, Nicole felt as though she were melting from the sun.

Across from the Loews Victoria movie house, Nicole and Eddie leaned against a red Buick as the sax player sipped a bottle of soda. Despite the heat, Eddie was dressed in an immaculate linen suit, although he had removed the narrow tie and opened the starched shirt's top buttons. "What's the problem, Nicole?" he asked. He couldn't tell if she was sluggish from the high temperature, angry at the world, or a combination of the two. "You wouldn't be hiding anything from me, would ya?"

With nervous eyes Nicole surveyed the kaleidoscopic activity of the boisterous boulevard, perturbed by the unrelenting noise of the neighborhood. Across the avenue, trifling Red Jackson and his reefer-mad crew of crazies danced wildly in front of Big Daddy's Record Rack.

"Looks like the heat has made the natives restless," Nicole commented. Pausing momentarily, Red Jackson stared at her pretty face and winked. "I don't know, Eddie," she said, shaking her head. "I just don't know." Even with her back turned, she could feel Red's eyes lingering over her body. "I know this is supposed to be the best week of our lives, but I feel so scared and confused. Everything feels so crazy, you know?" The loud blast of exploding Chinese firecrackers echoing from across the street almost made her burst into tears; just another one of Red Jackson's cronies playing the fool.

Eddie wiped his greasy hands on a napkin before throwing it amongst the debris in the dirty street. "Let's get out of this damn heat, it's starting to remind me of home," he said, climbing into the sleek convertible. "Another reason my black ass left Georgia; never did care for no whole lotta heat."

Casually driving a few blocks east, Eddie stopped in front of an ice cream shop called Snookie's Sugar Bowl. The cool air caressed their faces, comforting them after all the hours in the sun taking the photo for the album cover. Once they'd copped a squat, a slender server approached their table and gave them two glasses of ice water. "Hot enough for you?"

"Hey, Slim Goody," Eddie chuckled. "Give us two chocolate sundaes." Glancing across the stained Formica table, he noticed that Nicole seemed to be floating through a vast sky of her own thoughts. "You ain't doing drugs, is you, Nicole?"

If her stare was poisoned arrows, he would have been one dead sax player. "We've been in the studio three days and I'm not feeling the spirit of the music, Eddie. You would think I'd be excited about recording my album. Shit, it's something I've thought about for years. But . . . what is this stuff we're recording anyway? I'll tell you what it's *not*. It's not the blues. And that little motherfucker Willy is like a black dictator, a Negro Hitler if you ask me."

"Well, so what? You have a problem with Johnny Mercer and George Gershwin? We getting paid, right?"

"Yeah, we getting paid, but is that all that matters?" she asked. "We was getting paid singing the blues, playing music that made people feel a little something. This orchestra shit is like saccharine. There's no fire there, just stardust. It's like he wants me to be Patti Page or Kay Starr. Fucking Peggy Lee sounds blacker than me!

"Tomorrow we're supposed to record 'Nothing Lasts Forever.' I wrote that damn song for a small combo, but have you seen what he's done to it? You've seen those arrangements. That song is supposed to be raw, not sentimental. Just because it's a love song doesn't mean it has to be so damn syrupy."

"Look, baby girl, Bessie Smith been dead a long time now. Ain't nobody buying those kind of records no more. Some of these gutbucket folks in Harlem might still dig those sounds on the weekend, because it remind them of their distant country roots," Eddie reasoned, "but ain't nobody laying down any change in the record shops to take it home. You wanna perform for fags and gangsters forever?"

"It's not about where I sing, it's what I sing. Those fags and gangsters, they love what I do!" she screamed. "Then, to make things worse, Willy is starting to drop hints that I need a man in my life. Maybe even a husband. That would make Michelle very happy if I showed her a picture of me and my boyfriend in *Ebony*. It's bad enough already the way we argue over almost anything. She can be such a jealous person."

"You have more dames on the side than I do, sis. Why's a little picture-taking with a man going to be a problem?" Nicole frowned and playfully tossed a few ice cubes in his lap. "Look, we just have one more day in the studio, so let's make the best of it. Tell you what, after the session tomorrow, me, you, and Michelle will go over to The Secret and celebrate. Drink champagne, smoke reefer and stumble home. Would you like that?"

"Yeah, I'd like that."

"All right, good. Now, let's just worry about doing what we do."

Despite what Willy Harris requested, Nicole decided to bring Michelle to the studio with her. Eddie noticed Michelle sitting silently in the control booth dressed in Capri pants and a loose men's shirt that still looked feminine on her slender body. She was obviously amazed at all the stuff that went into making a record.

Gazing through the window of the control booth, Willy fought the impulse to stare at Michelle with disdain. He hated her and all she represented and all the mess she might be to them later. At lunch break, before the musicians returned to the studio, Willy confronted Nicole in the narrow hallway. Resting his leather briefcase on the floor, he grabbed her arm roughly. "You just refuse to act right, is that it? You want us all to suffer for your sins?"

"Sins?" she answered. "The only sin I see is you holding my arm like you my daddy. If you have a problem with something, why don't you just say it out loud?"

"It's not just my problem, Nicole," spat Willy. "You must not have seen the *Lenox Observer* this week. It's all about you and your kind." Releasing her arm, Willy opened his briefcase and withdrew copies of all the musical arrangements for their entire week of sessions. On top of the sheet music was a copy of the newspaper, which he threw at her. "If this were a different time, they would stone you to death or burn you at the stake. And I'll tell you one thing, no disc jockey is going to play a record from a woman who fucks other women. Like the paper says, it's unnatural."

"I think you know as much about being unnatural as I do!" she yelled. "You know how we abominations can tell when another one is in the room."

"I'll have you know, I am a married man with two kids, both boys." Chewing on his cigar as though it were a doggie biscuit, he yelped, "Don't you understand this is our big chance? You think I spent all this money and put work into this project so you could blow it all by being a freak of nature? Last I heard, it was sex appeal that sold records, not bull daggers.

Remember, Little Miss Confused, we do have a contract. I can make you jump through rings of fire if I choose."

Heading back into the studio, Nicole felt numb. She wanted to cry, but no tears came.

"You all right, sis?" asked Eddie. "We're getting ready to do your number, so let's make it tight."

"Let's take it from the top, gentlemen," Willy snipped from the control booth. "The tape is rolling."

Removing the piano intro in deference to the crying sound of violins, the studio was soon transformed into a make-believe ballroom: a hi-fi paradise where silky moonlight lasted forever and doves soared across the sky; the ballroom was a classy joint, where couples swayed to soft strings and atmospheric bass and Eddie's sax solo filled the studio with jazzy rhythmic undertones.

Yet, even with a honeyed arrangement, Nicole could not contain her pain. A shroud of sadness clouded her face. Closing her eyes, Nicole's tortured voice possessed them: seductive yet brutal. Her phrasings were scorching yet fragile. Her words were whiskey-laced, but her tongue had never been more sober.

Slowly approaching the chorus of "Nothing Lasts Forever," she opened her eyes. Staring through the cigarette haze, she looked directly into the control booth and sweetly sang, "But I love you / yes, Michelle, I love you . . ." Eyebrows were raised, snickers were silenced, and the melody lingered on until reaching its dramatic coda.

In a single take, Nicole Rose had created one of the most compelling, haunting ballads of her generation. Even in Willy Harris's mind, after he spliced out the name Michelle from the master tape, "Nothing Lasts Forever" would be a timeless classic.

Afterwards, Nicole wordlessly gestured to Michelle in the control booth. No one, not even Willy Harris, said a word. Holding hands, the ladies silently walked out the door.

"Hey! Sister Rose!" screamed Eddie. Sitting on a wooden stool, he rested his sax in his lap. "Where you going, sis? Hey, sis!"

∂∞

Later that evening, Eddie drove around the humid Harlem streets in search of Nicole. Believing she might have retreated to the sanctuary of The Secret, he headed over to St. Nicholas Place. Trying to turn at One Hundred Forty-fifth, he found that the street was blocked by a sea of police cars and firetrucks with lights flashing.

"What's the problem, officer?" Eddie asked the young Negro cop directing traffic.

"You know these damn wild street niggers," snapped the cop harshly. "Get a little too much heat on 'em and they think that's their cue to start rioting in the streets. These the kinds of niggers that make whitey think we all insane. Hell, they done messed up that little social club down the block bad. Good thing the joint was closed at the time. Of course, nobody saw anything . . . Niggers!"

Leaving the car in the middle of the street, Eddie walked to The Secret. A rusty garbage can had been thrown through the window, the words QUEERS NOT HERE spray-painted on the door. Inside, towering firefighters were still extinguishing the remainder of the inferno that had destroyed the bar. Shattered glass and burned copies of the *Lenox Observer* lay discarded in the flooded doorway. Hearing laughter a few feet away, Eddie glanced across the street and noticed Red Jackson's gold tooth gleaming in the twilight.

Moving into a rooming house the following month, Eddie soon received a large package in the mail. Tearing open the manila envelope, he was surprised to find the album cover for Checkerboard Records' first release, *Nothing Last Forever*. Shot in smoky sepia tone, the exquisite image showed Eddie and Nicole leaning against the side of the sleek convertible. Looking at the picture, he smiled. Wherever Nicole might have run off to, he hoped she was doing well.

Born Again

by t'ai freedom ford

S he let me in. Naah. Wait. Better than that. She took me in. Just swallowed me whole. Like a shark, but not that violent. I mean, it wasn't violent at all—more like a baby being born backwards. That's how she pulled me in. Her first time, but she knew what she was doing. My first time, and lucky she knew what to do.

My joint was rock. And then she put the rubber on and it felt like a rocket. Felt like it was gonna explode. Which was a good feeling. I don't know what everybody else talking 'bout when they say they hate jimmies 'cause it block the feeling. I could feel everything and I wasn't even inside yet. I was between her legs and the hairs of her stomach was soft against my joint. And I could feel her breath making the few little hairs on my chest stand up. And I swear I could feel her thighs shaking a little bit. Probably scared 'cause it was her first time and my joint is kind of a monster. Not bragging or nothing, but what's real is real.

I ain't even know what I was packing until that day me, Rowdy, and Nook-Nook was kissing these hoes in the back staircase. We knew they was hoes 'cause they still wanted to make out with us even after we took 'em to the back staircase that nobody use except to take a piss or tag they name on the walls. Rowdy and Nook-Nook's girls had nice bodies but they grills was burnt. My girl, Marisol, was this fine-ass Puerto Rican hottie. She had body for days, plus her face was pretty enough to make you wanna wife her. But she was a ho for sure 'cause soon as we get up there, Rowdy's girl Chi-Chi was like, "Marisol, *mira* . . ." She pointed at the red spray paint on the wall that said: MARISOL IS A HO. Marisol just shrugged and then they all started giggling. So then me, Rowdy, and Nook started laughing too, probably 'cause we was nervous more than anything else.

Then all I hear is sneakers squeaking—Nook-Nook and Rowdy backing they girls up against the walls. Marisol is already posted up against the wall with her name in the background. She grabs the end of my T-shirt and says, "*Ven aqui, Flaquito.*" And I know from Spanish class and on the street that she's basically saying: "Bring your slim, sexy ass here." I start cheesing uncontrollably, which totally messes up the cool side that I was try'na show, but damn! She had her head cocked, and her long hair was pulled over one shoulder, and her eyes was just talking to me. My joint act like it had ears too and was about to bust out of my pants. When I press up against her to kiss her, my jammie must've stabbed her in the guts 'cause she pushed me back a little and looked down at the bulge behind my zipper with her eyes all wide. "Damn . . . Your shit is big!" Everybody just bust out laughing. My face got real hot, but I tried to play cool. I just shrugged and raised my eyebrow a little bit. Grabbed my joint real quick to put him in check and proceeded to tongue Marisol's fine ass down.

That's how I found out my joint was a monster. 'Cause if Marisol the ho says your joint is big, then it is. 'Nuff said. And after we made out, like a couple of days later, I started getting all these funny looks from chicks. I mean, I'm used to getting looks 'cause I'm nice on the courts, but these looks was on another level. The bold ones would just come up to me and give me they phone number on a little bitty piece of loose-leaf paper. And that's all good for getting my freak on. But Nina, the one who let me in, is different.

Nina is like the red leaves on the trees now that school's starting back. 'Cause the green ones is a dime a dozen, and the yellow ones is all over the place, but the red ones—the red ones is special. And Gooma says, "Special is the fingerprint of God." I ain't never really know what she was talking about till I seen Nina smile. She make you believe in a God and that He had everything to do with making her as beautiful as she is.

Nina is butterfly beautiful. And you don't hardly see butterflies in the ghettos of Brooklyn 'cause ain't no flowers or nothing for them. But when you do see one, you wanna catch it. You wanna hold onto something so pretty. You wanna make it yours. But butterflies are hard to catch. I've been close, but only wound up with gold dust on my fingers.

In the fifth grade, we went on this field trip to the Natural History Museum to see the butterfly exhibit. And I remember thinking, *How gay is that?* Going to see some dead butterflies. But I ain't care 'cause it was a chance to get out of class. We get there and there's this glass room (look like it was cut straight out of the rain forest and brought to New York), and there's butterflies everywhere. All the girls was like, "Ohmygod, ohmygod, lookit, lookit," pushing they greasy fingers into the glass.

Finally our group goes in. The room is mad hot and funny-smelling, kind of like the train platform in the summer. That kind of heat where you don't even wanna breathe 'cause you afraid that your lungs might catch on fire. But yo! The butterflies was out of control, yo! So many different colors and I ain't even know how big some of them could be. And one of the signs said some of them only have a life span of a couple of weeks. Which made me think how brothers is kind of like butterflies 'cause some of us be on the streets with a two-week life span too. Never know when you might end up dust on somebody's fingers, your wings broken for being too fly for niggas to handle.

Some of the girls held they fingers out so that the butterflies could land. The dudes just took them off the plants and put them on girls' shoulders. I was standing there looking at all the color and thinking how God must be an artist. Gooma always say: "You get your creativity from the Creator." At least that's what she tell me when I be bragging on how I be in the lane with three punks in my face and I just find a way to make the ball go in. "Glory be to God," Gooma say. And so I was just standing there giving Him props, wondering if this is how Heaven looks, when people is pointing at me. I look at my shirt and there's this big-ass butterfly, but it kind of looks like a moth 'cause the wings on the outside are dark brown. But when it opened its wings, my mouth opened with it 'cause the colors— green, blue, yellow—was amazing.

Nina's like that butterfly. Landed on me so sweet and gentle that I ain't even notice her until the day she opened up her wings and showed me her colors. All I could think was, *Glory be to God.*

Between her legs, I couldn't help thinking the same thing. And she was shaking like a puppy taken from her mother. I was just hard. I mean stiff like a white boy in a dance hall. The jimmy was on and my joint was ready. Nina's brown eyes was on me—intense like my eyes on the ball when I'm try'na force a turnover. Her eyes looked like little fires try'na burn through me. Same fires I saw when we first met.

Last year, we had just got back from spring break, which ain't nothing but a week of playing handball or dicing in the hallway, 'cause ain't like we going to some beach in Florida where a bunch a white people smelling like coconut is running around drinking beers. I remember it was second-period biology and I was dozing 'cause Mr. Piggle was explaining the mating process of frogs and I figured I'd pay attention when he got to humans. I was in the back with my head against the cool black lab table when she came in.

A girl's voice with a Southern accent asked, "'Scuse me, is this Mr. Piggly's class?" The class's laughing woke me up a little, but not enough to raise my head and see what was going on.

"That's Piggle, my dear. Mr. Piggllle," he said, riding the "l" sound. "Indeed, you are in the right place. However, we're almost to capacity, but there is an opening next to Mr. Johnson." The class started laughing again, but there's two Johnsons so I didn't look up. "He's the one napping in the back. Perhaps you can get him to pay attention . . ."

By the time I looked up, she was sitting down in the chair next to me. I wiped the slob from my face and opened my eyes wider to make sure I wasn't dreaming or something. Her eyes was reddish-brown like the fires we used to make at camp, and just like that my face felt hot. She smiled at me and I could've sworn I was standing at the gates, 'bout to be let into Heaven.

She put my joint in her. Not all at once, but easing me in a little, then a little more. It was warm, warm like the butterfly room. When I got totally in, I felt like I was being hugged by God.

She had one hand on my stomach and the other on my ass, guiding me in and out slow until I found my rhythm. I got into it quick and then watched her to see if I was doing it right. Her face looked like a jigsaw puzzle of pain and confusion and some missing piece I hadn't found yet. I pushed deeper, trying to find that piece with the smile on it. She sucked in her breath and made a sound like a scared snake.

"It hurt?" I asked her, 'cause my joint is kind of big and it was her first time and I was digging pretty deep.

"A little . . . I'm okay," she whispered, but it wasn't really a whisper, more like she was try'na catch her breath.

I eased out a little so I wouldn't rip her shit up. I heard about girls getting they twats pulled out of shape by dudes, and Nina's was so perfect and tight that I ain't wanna bust it out like that the first time.

"Yeah, like that." She pushed and pulled me so that my rhythm was short and quick. My joint was halfway in and out. And after a few more strokes, the rocket was ready to blast. *Ten, nine, eight* . . . Her head was back, her mouth open, her eyes closed, her face looked peaceful, not like it was hurting or nothing. *Seven, six* . . . My stomach felt like a cage with butterflies flying around. My mouth was full of drool 'cause it felt so good I could taste it. *Five, four* . . . Nina's little bed squeaked. She was breathing fast, letting out these little sounds that I guess was a good thing. *Three, two* . . . And the rocket was out of here. Blasted off into space, sucked up into some faraway galaxy with no oxygen. And I couldn't breathe for like three seconds, but it felt like three seconds to a drowning man. And then this hot liquid overflowed out my mouth and down my chin like lava from a volcano. It was only slob though—a long line of slob connected from my bottom lip to the crease between Nina's stomach and thigh. She opened her eyes and wiped my spit off. Then she scooted back on the sheets so that my joint just plopped on the bed like it had been shot. And I could feel myself slowly floating back to Earth like a burnt-out balloon that slipped out of some little kid's hand. And the butterflies wasn't in my stomach no more, but must've been flying out of my mouth 'cause my lips felt like they could speak poetry.

"Damn . . ." was the only thing that I could say though. Not a disappointed "damn" like seeing a girl with a dope body who turns out to be ugly, but a overwhelmed "damn," like when you see a rainbow for the first time.

Nina wiped my chin with her thumb and laughed. I felt stupid. Her wiping my slob made me feel like a baby. Made me feel helpless like I had shitted in my diaper and now had to marinate in it. My joint felt like a baby too. All cold and shriveled and abandoned like a newborn in a dumpster. I wanted to be surrounded by the warmth of her again. I wanted to be born again. 'Cause really, that's what it was like. She gave me new life.

"And so she gave him life anew. Resurrected him, so to speak," says Sista Wummi, this new teacher we got for Social Studies who wears her head wrapped and all these colorful African clothes and don't like to be called Miss. She just finished telling us about this Isis chick. This Egyptian lady whose husband Osiris had got cut up into like forty pieces on some old ill shit. The cats who cut him up put his body parts in different places or something. But Isis found all the parts of her man. Well, all except the most important part—his jammie. This nigga Osiris must've been the bomb with the sexing 'cause old girl searched all over the world for his shit. When she couldn't find it, she made him one and then gave him some of her energy and spirit and brought the brother back to life.

We leave class and Rowdy and Nook-Nook is talking shit in the hallway, which is crowded and noisy. Cats huddled around a radio blaring beats while they kick freestyles, girls with headphones on soloing their favorite singer loud as hell, and everybody yelling at each other like it's normal.

Rowdy adds to the noise. "Bitches these days wish they had some powers like that." Rowdy is just that: rowdy. Real name: Rodney. The type of brother that likes the way glass sound against the pavement. The one who bust caps not firecrackers on the Fourth of July. The fool who doesn't start fights, just finishes them with a Timbo boot to the skull.

Nook-Nook gives Rowdy some dap. "I'm saying, yo. Bringing a nigga back to life?!" Nook-Nook just is. Don't even know that fool's real name. Seriously, I mean, the teachers even call him Nook-Nook Jones. He 'bout one of the ugliest cats you wanna meet, but is known for getting in the panties.

"That bitch made a dick for that nigga, son!" Rowdy laughs.

"That's 'cause he was prob'ly banging that bitch silly, yo. She had to have it." Nook grabs his crotch.

"I'm saying, son, if a bitch wanna impress me, bring Biggie back, nah mean?" Rowdy crashes his fist against a locker, but the hallway is so loud that nobody notices.

Me, I don't say jack. Probably 'cause I know the power Nina has. Rowdy and Nook is always bragging about the girls they done banged, but they girls must not have the power like Nina. They girls all hoes anyway. Any power they had probably slipped out of they loose coochies a long time ago.

"So, Man, what up wit you and Nina?" Nook-Nook ask 'cause he be keeping tabs on the booty like that.

"What you mean 'what up'?" Our lockers is in the same area. I jook mines open, looking for my trig book.

"I'm saying, yo, did you tap that?" Nook waves his hand like a paddle.

"Yeah . . . I hit it." I smile to hide the fact that I'm not really digging this line of questioning.

Rowdy leans back and kicks a dent into his locker, diagonally below mines, and jumps in on the double-team. "So how was it?"

"It was aiight," I lie. I mean, am I s'posed to tell them that I was born again? That a ugly old caterpillar like me made love to a butterfly? They wouldn't even begin to comprehend what I was talking about. It's been two days since the rebirth and I'm still try'na figure it out.

Nook-Nook and Rowdy look at me like I stole something. The bell rings for fourth-period trigonometry and I pray that they leave it at that.

"We late," I say to distract them.

"Nigga, we always late," Nook-Nook say.

"Fuck trig! I'm 'bout to get with that real math in the bathroom over by Mr. Munson class." Rowdy grins and shakes his hand like there's dice inside.

"Oh word?" Nook-Nook seem interested, but I got to keep a C average to stay in the game so I know I'm going to class.

"Craps. Y'all down?" Rowdy pulls out a small knot and counts it right in the middle of the hallway almost like a dare.

"Naah . . . you be playing with the ballers . . ." Nook start walking again and I follow like the masses followed Moses.

"Broke niggas stay broke . . ." Rowdy shoves his money in his front pocket and bumps fists with me and Nook before cutting the corner.

Nook mumble, "Dumb niggas stay dumb . . ." He sound like a ghetto commercial for the Board of Education. Really, it sound like something Gooma would say, but without the *nigga*.

℘

In class, Mr. Fishbein is reviewing the quadratic equation and half the students is already nodding 'cause the room is hot as hell. Some cats is using they book covers as fans. The other half of the class is nodding 'cause they know they ain't ever gon' need this math junk in real life. I'm kind of in a daze try'na figure out how I can use this formula to calculate all the money I'm gon' make when I go pro.

Nook shoves a piece of folded paper in front of me. On the inside of the fold it says, *How it smell?* I sniff the room, which smells like stale chalk and musk. I shrug.

He snatch the paper back, scribble, and pass it again. It say, *Her pussy*, underlined twice. I look at him like he ride the little yellow bus 'cause I know he ain't talking 'bout Nina, and I know he don't expect me to answer. His eyes look like they 'bout to pop out of his head if I don't say something.

But I don't remember smelling anything. Barely remember seeing anything but Nina's body and the fire in her eyes. Thinking 'bout it again, I start to see all the little things I was too stiff to notice.

Nina actually live in a house—not the projects, not a walk-up, not a co-op, not a duplex, but a house—with her moms and pops. Oh, she got a little brother too. They from Atlanta and it just so happen that the family was going back down to visit they grandmother or something. Nina couldn't go 'cause she was in summer school taking a math course so she could graduate on time. They trusted her to stay, I guess 'cause she seventeen. Just asked her aunt to come check on her while they was gone, but her aunt is a nurse who work nights, which left me the perfect opportunity to be all up in the crib.

Even right around the corner from the projects, they house is nice enough. Wall-to-wall carpet, the first thing I noticed 'cause Nina made me take off my shoes and it felt good under my feet. Not like the cold dingy linoleum we got in our apartment. Wood paneling all over the place and plastic-covered furniture and brass lamps and pictures hanging everywhere. Nina with ponytails and ice cream. Nina and her brother at the beach playing with a lump of sand. Nina's dad with a fly collar shirt on and a Afro, her mom pregnant with Nina's head against her belly.

Nina's room was nice like some shit off some TV show or something.

Pink walls and a bedspread with matching sheets and pink lace curtains. Some real white-girl shit. Most of these project girls got the same pale green walls everybody else got. Chipped and peeling and covered with posters pulled out of magazines of they favorite rappers. Mismatch sheets, pillow with no pillowcase. Old mattress that been peed on by everybody and smell like it.

Nina even had her own bathroom. A second bathroom would be nice to have in my apartment since my mother always be smoking our bathroom out. I used Nina's bathroom after I blasted. Flower wallpaper, soap shaped like roses, and a towel to dry your hands. Nice. I was nosy. Opened the medicine cabinet. She was neat. Little bottles of perfume and nail polish all lined up. Some headache medicine and bobby pins. Under the sink a box of pads, some tampons, and a pink box with a white woman in a field with a towel wrapped around her. The box said: *Sweet Love. Essence of Strawberry. Disposable Douche.* Ill. I had heard Rowdy and Nook talk about girls whose coochie stank like the Korean fish market and how they needed Massengill or some other brand of douche that I felt like they knew way too much about. But then again, they both got sisters.

Strawberries. It was all coming back to me but in patches, kind of like when Mr. Munson started using Rogaine. Did it really smell like strawberries? It didn't smell like rotten fish.

Nook-Nook makes some kind of whining sound and cocks his head at me like a dog try'na let his owner know he gotta go. He waits for a answer. Do he really need to know all of that 'bout my butterfly? I mean, he my boy and all, but dag. But he was the one to school me in the ways of women. Told me how to use jimmies to keep my balls from falling off. Guess I owe him that much info.

So I tell him. Well, write it on the paper: *strawberries.* He grins, shaking his head like he knows exactly what I'm talking 'bout, and balls up the paper. I wipe the sweat from my forehead and try to concentrate on what Mr. Fishbein is talking 'bout, 'cause I'm not try'na be the dumb nigga who stays dumb.

Knot Frum Hear

by D. Scot Miller

S helving books at the store last night, the letter from Sham Black fell out of a worn copy of *Dhalgren*:

Bards,

I know that all of you kept journals of our travels. I know because I saw you there, scribbling in your little rowboats as I was in mine. And when the seven of us, always seven different, stepped out on those unknown, heavily populated docks, we may have seen different things in those markets and bazaars. We may have heard the same language and spoke in different ones. Who is to say besides us? It can be agreed, I pray, that there are lands on this land that humans cannot tread nor see.

I'm writing this to you from a café in a cyclopean cavern. You have to walk along cathedral space fractal networks, labyrinthine gargantuan tunnels, until you come to this cove that captures rays of sun from above and spotlights the little tables that remind of Paris back in the day. It's breathtaking. I can hear the lapping of one of the many slow black underground rivers, and slim waterfalls plunging down smooth rock. Who dug this hollow earth beneath the ice foreseen by Poe?

Trade consists of occasional precious gems and cultivation of high-grade bud, every sort of magic mushroom, and, I have just learned, white poppy. The town belongs officially to America of Tomorrow, so I'm inclined to believe that the Nazis must have had some hand in the initial construction. These days most of the natives are shiftless ne'er-do-wells on the dole. Deep cave tribal country lies just across the lake. Riffraff, artists, drug addicts, sorcerers, smugglers, and perverts live in the crumbling hotels half encrusted with pale green vines, along the lakefront, an avenue of squalid cafés, gem emporia, noodle shops, vlaamse frites stands, and occult bookstores.

When I came in on the pier, I thought that I'd reached Interzone. A few people were bathing along the black beach, and honest-to-God fifties-style tourists, complete with flashbulb cameras and black sandals and white socks, were gawking at this shrine behind their bazaar, where pallid old Tong pamongs tranced out on fungus drool and rolled their eyes. I breathed in the heavy fumes of incense; everything seemed meaningful and menacingly bright. You know how it goes.

I've rented the same room that Brother Hakim Bey wrote his missives in. It's above a bait shop. Life among the Trogs is mostly rural sloth and degenerate superstitious rites of sensual abandon, the larval and unhealthy mysteries of chthonic mutants. To think that America of Tomorrow, with its pristine though terminally earthbound flying cars, and musty though forever sanitized keep in the center of Main Street, had a hand in this beautiful monstrosity of a city planning!

Caveboy gangs huddle in the corners and alleyways, marking walls and smoking those god-awful frop cigarettes. More dangerous are the maverick Wildboys in silver jockstraps and roller skates cutting through the streets. To look in the eyes of one of those enfants terrible is to see a complete evolutionary uprising. I may travel with them to Interzone.

Check it out, I just found out that there's an airport on Surface 23 that can fly me to Interzone. An airplane, can you believe it?

Strikin. All feet. All Soul.
Sham

Let me tell you how I met Sham Black.

West Virginia, Dunbar Junior High School football field, 123rd Annual Commode Bowl. Riverside Rats vs. the Hillside Rams.

Every Thanksgiving morning the men of Dunbar, on both sides of the railroad tracks that split through the town (Riverside and Hillside), begin to drink. At ten o'clock they stagger into their F-1s, Monte Carlos, and Firebirds ("Quality car there, buddy"), and honk their horns in a slow, drunken parade down Dunbar Avenue, cold beers in hand, until they reach the football field at the end of town near the river. Then they soak the field until it's nothing but a mud pool. Then they get drunk. Then they try to play football. I was sitting at the top of the bleachers nursing my father's flask for a pre-supper buzz.

"——," this black guy in a leather peacoat and blue-and-white striped wool hat said from the top of the bleachers.

"Pardon me."

He motioned me up to where he was sitting. I went up.

"They're doing a version of an ancient ritual. Early agricultural tribes had orgies in the fields right before planting. It was supposed to be good for both the crops and the tribe. Been around for thousands of years."

"Who are you, Mr. Wizard? Looks like a bunch of drunk rednecks rolling in the mud to me."

"Just because they don't know they do it don't mean they ain't doing it. I've a feeling that somebody back a hundred years ago knew. See that guy over there?"

He pointed to "Big" John Gillaspell, town paralytic, who had just taken off his mud-covered shirt and was spinning it around over his head like a helicopter blade. His sagging basketball shorts were caked to blackness, and contrasted starkly with the fish-belly paleness of the fifteen pounds of flaccid flab flapping and swaying side to side in his drunken victory stumble upfield.

"Whooooooooo!" Big John wailed until a ball of phlegm choked him to a silent, hobbit-like trot.

"That guy and his good wife are going to go home tonight full of beer and hubris. He is not going to bathe and she's not going to ask him to. They're going to put on their favorite soul album and they're going to roll around in all that dirt and mud. They're going to fuck—"

I laughed. No, I guffawed, loud and drunken.

"They're going to fuck like they haven't in three hundred sixty-four days. And tomorrow morning they'll feel cleaner, stronger, and clearer than they have since last year, without shame, long before they've showered and changed the sheets. And come the next harvest cycle a new crop of football players and plant workers will be born, with a healthy green field to play, drink, and fuck on. It's been that way for a long, long time. There's a lot going on behind the veil."

I took another sip from my flask and let the Rapid Cur warm away the chill. I liked the way he talked. I wanted to talk like that one day. The words just coming out like that and shit. I would have definitely talked more if I could have talked like that back then.

"Pez?"

"Yeah, thanks. Yo man, what is that?!"

"Tupac Pez dispenser. You don't get these?"

"That is so dope! Hell no."

"They got Biggie too. Want another one?"

"Thanks. That is too ill."

"Been making them for nearly twenty years where I'm from."

"Where you from?"

"Knot Frum Hear."

"I know that. But where you from?"

He just smiled at me. "Hey, you smoke la?"

"Huh?"

"Herbs. You indulge in sacred herbs?"

"Naw, man. And I don't know nobody either."

"I'm not looking. I'm saying I got smoke." He pulled out a fat joint and lit it right there. At the top of the bleachers. In front of everybody.

"What are you doing?!" I started to get up. It was the stinkiest pot I'd ever smelled in my life. Smelt like someone was brewing a batch of skunk tea.

"The cops are right there, man. You're on your own, partner. I don't even know you."

"It's cool, man, this ain't weed, frop." He coughed. "Look." He blew a cloud of smoke in the direction of the cluster of plaid parka-wearing WallMall shoppers.

They didn't even turn their heads. Cautiously, I watched him collect another cloud of thick gray smoke in his cheeks and expel it. The smoke hung heavy and deliberate over the crowd.

"Besides, nobody round here would have the imagination to do this. You cats still smoking dirt out this way, this isn't anywhere near weed to these people. Wouldn't be nothing to you if I hadn't've told you. And nobody smokes weed in the bleachers, right? So, I'm nobody right now. Get it? Have a seat, little brother, and hit this."

I reached for it. He handed it over, let me get the sticky cigarette to my lips.

"Before you take a hit, understand this: Only *I* am nobody. You are somebody. They are everybody else. That's your nature, their nature, and my preference. I repeat, you are not nobody or everybody, so you will not do the things that nobody does or the things that everybody does. Rather, you will do the things that nobody does not do nor everything that everybody does. You are somebody, not nobody, and damn sure ain't everybody. See what I'm saying?"

"You're saying I am somebody."

"Say it!"

"I AM—"

"Say it!"

"SOMEBODY!"

"Yes!"

We both laughed and I took a deep pull of the joint and began to cough immediately. They were deep, deep coughs that seemed to start in my stomach and wrench from my lungs. I couldn't catch my, catch my, breath. And, and, I felt my throat constrict as my tongue strained from mouth, mouth, my mouth. Spittle and snot sprayed from every hole in my head, my head. I gagged, gagged, gagged, gagged, and emptied the contents of my stomach through the slats below my feet onto the gravel.

"See," he said, rubbing my back. "You were thinking you were nobody. You are somebody, only *I* am nobody. For you, hitting that like me made you sick. Nobody smokes like me. Work with nobody and everybody will never know. If you want to be somebody, remember that."

"Who-are-you, fuck, man, man?"

"Sham, Black, Black Sham Black." He extended his leather-clad arm, stuck out his hand, still wearing that smile.

I shook it, trying to get a glimpse of his tattoo.

"Hey, scene seen one won of these deez before for?" He held out his forearm. The tattoo was the outline of a black heart. The crowns curved slightly into curlicues at the top with roots forming a base at the bottom.

"Yeah, Janet Jackson's got one on her ass."

"It's on her back, but butt you ewe seen it be four right write?"

"Yeah."

"How many thymes?"

"Shit, I don't know. A couple dozen."

"No whut it is?"

"It is what it is. Nope."

"It's a Sankofa. An Adinkra symbol from the ancient language of the Akan people of Ghana. It means, 'Go back and fetch it.' Means go back and reclaim the past passed, dig? Get the essence of the culture's knowledge and wisdom and use it as a tool for the future. How many times you seen it?"

"I would say, excluding *The Velvet Rope*, four. But I've heard that word before. How you say it?"

"Sankofa."

"Yeah, I've heard that word before somewhere. Man, that's some good shit. Got me all paranoid. That word scares the shit out of me."

"There's a reason for that. Great horrors were done to the place and the people to put that kind of poison into The Word word. Sankofa. Look it up, millions of people were slaughtered in and around the word The Word so you'll get psychically ill eel when you here it. Isn't that fucked up? This," he pointed at his tattoo, "came first. But when eye say The Word you don't hear 'Go back and fetch it' here, you see images of the Holocaust. Which would discourage you from going back and fetching it, even if ewe new, huh? Why would somebody want to do that?"

"Could be a coincidence."

"No, it wasn't."

"You like my pops, huh? He doesn't believe in coincidences either."

"I believe in coincidences, just that they can be planned."

"What the fuck that mean?"

"Living without a creation myth contributes to the subtle but pervasive quality of disorientation in modern life as anomie: the sense of not fitting in, which is an inescapable condition of those who have no conception of what they are supposed to fit into. That's about alienation. I red it in a book called *Maps of Time* by a scientist named David Christian. You read?"

"Well, yeah."

"You seem ashamed that you read."

"I'm not ashamed of shit, man." I went to take another sip when I realized that I didn't need it. I was higher than giraffe pussy.

"Ever read *Fahrenheit 451?*"

"Bradbury, sure."

"What if someone thought that instead of getting rid of the books, getting rid of the readers would be more cost effective? Readers write books, right? These daze with all the word processors and voice-activated pages—"

"I never heard of that," I say.

"It's knew. You can speak into a mic and the words just print out on the page."

"Cool."

"Yeah, but writing is going to get easier and easier. There are going to be more and more books out there, more than ever before. Too many! Too many books, can you believe it? So many books coming so fast that you can't tell what's enriching and what's draining you, making you tired. The hard thing is going to be the reading. Remembering what *we* do it for, you *know?*"

"Yeah." I looked up at him. I did know what he meant. I really knew. For a second, it was like we were in a vacuum and it was just me and him. I really *looked* at him. He looked like a hairy version of my dad. Strong jaw, covered in a trimmed beard, smiling at me. This nigga loved me. Loved me in such a way that I'd never felt before or since. It wasn't a sexual thing or anything like that. It was some deep shit, like the kind of love you get for someone after being pinned down in some shit together, but deeper. That's what I saw in those eyes, when I felt what he meant when he said "reading."

He stood and stretched.

"Well youngblood, nice meeting you." He was about to leave me, stoned, on the bleachers thinking about these mud-covered puds having hot brown love.

I remember seeing the orgy taking place before my eyes. The muddy-breasted men rolling over each other in a slick tangle for the ball, their wives and children screeching from the sides in bacchanalian frenzy. The center bending, the QB mounting, and the clashing of wet muddy flesh beginning anew. Satyrs and nymphs poking, licking, prodding, grunting like pigs, braying like mules, barking, wailing in the mud, officiated by Ted from the Stop & Shop who provided the kegs and his own whistle.

"Okay, Sham. See you around?" I wanted to tell him that I noticed that all of the players were semi-erect, but what the fuck would that have sounded like?

"Probably not. Say, do you swim?"

"Doggy paddle."

"Not good enough. Living off a river like this, you could really learn how to swim."

"Sounds good." It did.

"All soul. All feet." And he walked off the bleachers and out of Dunbar forever.

March 17, 1999

Tyro is a sixty-year-old cat with no legs and one arm. Claims he was a Green Beret in 'Nam. He lives in one of the residential hotels on Jefferson. Every store is burnt out, except the liquor store, the porno shop, and Circ Sev Books where I've been working for the last six years. All the cats are making it to his crib. The Riders watch his gate. Black-and-whites, beat cops, and unmarked boxy sedans: They all cruise through like no one knows what they're looking for. The block has been occupied for nearly a week. There's some cats rapping out front. They hang out at the store sometimes. I nod to them. Hit the buzzer and wait.

"It all comes down to milk."

"Milk."

"Yeah. If you're a mammal, you create white milk. Mother's milk is always white. White? Milk? Purity? Get it?"

"No."

"Mother's milk is *light* in the *crucible*." He poked the side of his temple with an index finger. I'd never noticed it before, but homeboy was cock-eyed. "You can't let the *brown*, the *dark*, mix with *white* milk. In there, milk is all that's good." He looks over at me. "They've confused light with white. It's a linguistic confusion. You see? White is the absence of all color while light is the presence of all colors and then some, but on that *deeper* level, you dig? They've got that shit all—"

"Nigga, you crazy," his boy interrupted.

"Maybe, but I tell you what, motherfuckers will go to some extremes just to keep they truth true. Moscone was the monkey in the middle. What you think, youngblood?" They looked at me.

"Well, metaphors define reality," I say.

"True."

"Word is bond! See? That's what I'm sayin' . . ." The door buzzed and I left them at the gate.

An old woman escorts me up the stairs to Tyro. I've got his special order of Clarence Major's *Dictionary of Afro-American Slang* in a paper bag with a piece of tape holding it closed. I couldn't find it anywhere on the web. Ended up having to call The Pig in the City. They knew a collector who was being gentrified out of his flat: twenty-five dollars. I tell myself that Tyro can't have this one on credit. He just can't.

The light from the one dusty window in his room is cut with shadows from the fire escape and recedes across my skim of faces and paper. There are five guys in the room. Three sit on the faded green sofa bed, sipping something out of plastic red cups with white rims. I'd never seen them before, but they nod to me and I nod back. I've seen the two other brothers slumped on stools at the dingy yellow kitchenette counter around the way, so I nod to them too. Tyro's room is full of paper, the walls covered with maps and blueprints. Every corner is crammed with books, manuals, loose-leaf, legal pads, and journals. He works hard at keeping the place tidy, but the papers spill out from under the sofa bed, collect on top of the black-and-white television on the rollaway stand, and sprout in index cards and cookie fortunes around the red shag carpeting, worn flat. He looks like a chocolate Fidel with his long gray beard and faded fatigues as the door opens.

"—Henry Dumas. You cats have got to get into Dumas. We were there in Harlem in sixty-eight, man. During the riots. Just come back to the world and had something. We put it down for a minute, right on. There's some things about those times they ain't telling you. We were doing more than those cats could imagine. They gunned that brother down in the street! You hear me? Unarmed, on a subway platform, assassinated. May 23, 1968, one month and nineteen days after they killed the King. Killed Bobby Hutton right down the street from here two days after. Seventeen bullets. Don't tell me that they don't fear the Word. Nommo is real. Say it. I'll tell you like I told them. I believe I was spared so I could come back and tell this.

"Okay, the cat that found me was hit himself, but he didn't seem to care. He looked me in the eye . . . for a long time. My legs were busted up from a grenade. This V.C.—that's Viet Cong, youngblood—stood over me. I could tell he was thinking something. He raised his rifle. I kept looking at him in the eye. It was one of the few times my prayers were answered. The cat suddenly turned and ran off. He had shot several of my buddies already, but he let me go.

"All I can figure is that one day the chips are all coming down. America is gonna have to face the yellow race. Black and yellow might have to put their hands together and bring this thang off. You cats out in the street, learn to fade fast. Learn to strike hard, but don't be around for the explosion. If you don't organize you ain't nothing but a rioter, a scavenger, a penny-ante crook. These mothers won't hesitate to put a cap in your ass.

"I ain't saying you should get off the street. I know like you know. Uncle means you know ultimate good, brothers. Take it for what it's worth. I'm laying it down like it is. I got it from the eagle's beak. That's the way he speak. Get the Man out of our neighborhood. I used to say 'Whitey,' but you know what? Uncle Tom's alive and well, dig? Keep women and children off the streets. Don't riot. Rebel. You cats got this message. Do what you got to do. Stick together and listen for the Word to come. Obey it."

"What you mean by 'fade,' old dude? Where the fuck we supposed to run? They got cameras everywhere."

Two of the guys laughed. Must have been his boys.

"*Read*, little brother. I ain't talking about just *hiding*. I'm talking about fading. Read Dumas, *Ark of Bones*. Then come back and see me. Not to mention, look at you with that phone on your hip. Every last one of you cats with one of those on, you might as well be wearing a bell around your neck. GPS, Global Positioning Systems, huh? You think that little map in your whips is all that. You bragging 'cause you don't have to call an operator when you get a flat tire. What do you think that is?"

That's when they kicked in the door.

Armed to the teeth, and guns drawn. Soldiers in combat boots, black canvas cargo pants, bulletproof vests, and riot helmets pour into Ty's, shouting at us to remain calm. One of the three guys on the sofa reached inside his jacket and was knocked cold by a rifle butt. I have no idea what he was reaching for.

They began to check identification cards. When one of them grabbed mine, she took it over to the only one not wearing a helmet. He was blond with a buzz cut and a little earphone and mic. He spoke into his headpiece and looked over at me, nodding.

"All right," she said walking back over to me, "you come with us." She was smiling, trying to be cordial about it.

"What's this all about?"

Holding me by the arm, she helped me to my feet. "We've just got to get some more info. Won't take long at all." She smiled again, weaker this time.

"I'm not going anywhere till you tell me what the fu—"

The soldier in the doorway fell first. He was holding his crotch and moaning for his mama. Two more men and a woman fell. All holding themselves, rolling around on the dirty shag carpeting, moaning and groaning for Jesus.

Then it walked in. A robot made of empty soda cans, VCR parts, twine, and garbage can lids. Two girl doll heads, hanging from its waist and cupping its crotch, spat fire and vomited smoke. Flames sparked from its feet and throat. It held up a cumbersome girded arm, draped in a leopard skin, and pointed a pink toy pistol at the remaining soldier.

"Bop Gun, orgone accumulator. You'll be fine in a few hours," the robot said with a voice that sounded like metallic echo forced through a blender, and fired the weapon at the soldier's crotch.

Too scared to move, the SEAL fell over with crossed eyes and rolled around with his buddies on the floor.

"They're having the best orgasms of their lives right now." The robot addressed the doubly shocked onlookers. He pointed the Bop Gun at the leader of the three-man group. "Want some?"

"Naw, that's cool."

The robot nodded over to the vet. "Tyro."

"RAM-L, don't worry about the cleanup. I've got some tight brothers in The Town."

"Soul. You!" He pointed to me. "Come with me." I got up to follow him out of Tyro's.

"You got my book, brother?" Tyro was looking at me down the bridge of his nose, smiling. I tossed the bag to him.

"Solid."

"That's thirty-five, Ty."

"Damn! What? The thing made out of gold?"

"Might as well be. Cough it up."

Tyro looked at RAM-L, then back at me. "Come by next Friday and we'll be all square, cool?"

It was my turn to glance at the robot standing in the doorway, swiveling its flaming metal head up and down the hall, and then back at Ty.

"Next Friday, dammit."

I lumbered down the stairs behind RAM-L into the street.

I was expecting us to be surrounded when we came out. Instead, a single jeep sat outside, the engine still idling, with a twenty-year-old soldier boy sleeping at the wheel with a big smile on his face.

We walked down Jefferson, crossed on Twelfth, and headed up Harrison. Me and this seven-foot-tall steam-powered robot. No one seemed to notice. If they did, they acted like they didn't. It was as if everyone was under a spell. An act-like-you-don't-see-it-and-it's-not-there kind of spell. I kept my mouth closed and marveled at the silence inside the bubble his presence made.

I remembered watching some deaf kids talking to each other in sign language while waiting for a train once. They were moving their hands all fast, arguing about something. To me, it was like their hands were making a sound vacuum, sucking in all the noise around them with their active silence. Standing next to them, I felt like I was in that vacuum, and something inside me got very quiet. Like they'd sucked those random ramblings, mumbles, screams, and shouts out of my head, and I was just quiet. So quiet there, beside them.

It was like that walking next to RAM-L, except he was sucking in sight instead of sound. I was invisible. And that's a strange feeling. It's like people go on about their business. Like they're walking through you, because they don't acknowledge you, I guess. Something inside them just doesn't *feel* you. Like, if they were half-asleep in their bedrooms and I crept in and stood over them, their bodies wouldn't *feel* me there.

RAM-L's steps were slow and each move brought a symphony of clangs and tin crinkles. It was like walking in slow motion. I didn't want to speak. I thought I was dreaming, a little bit. I didn't want to break the spell.

We got to the Bank of America on Harrison and RAM-L stopped in front of an automatic teller machine. He stuck a finger into the card slot and twenty-dollar bills began to pour onto the sidewalk. My jaw dropped.

"Pick those up."

Didn't have to tell me twice. I counted at least seven thousand dollars. We lumbered for a little longer; I was too busy counting money to see where we were going.

"My chariot." I looked up from the money to find myself standing in front of a rusted Chevette hatchback.

"What the—"

The robot hit itself on the top of the head and collapsed. Its body just sunk to the ground next to the little boxy car. As metallic skin collected at its feet, a skinny brother in a wifebeater and a pair of boxer shorts emerged.

"RAM-L?!"

The man took off his wave cap and rubbed his pate. "It's Rammellzee. Hot as shit in there. Get in. Talk on the way."

I just stood there, the wad of money in my hand. I thought about ganking him, can't lie. But I figured, if he knew Ty, and trusted me enough to let me hold the cash, then this whole thing warranted further investigation. I got in. RAM-L ran to the back of the car, opened the hatch, picked up the robot crust, and tossed it in. It looked like his recycling: cans, bottles, string, and tubes. He was dressed by the time he got into the driver's seat.

"Where we going?"

"The City. Buckle up."

We sputtered and rolled into traffic.

There was a jam on the MAZE.

"Where we going?"

"Zero Group Three."

We careened out into the carpool lane.

"Let me ask you something." He looked over at me.

"Okay."

"How can a government be structured straight using a symbolic code subconsciously remanipulated and its symbols not belonging to the verbal formation?"

"I don't understand . . ." Nearly hitting a tollbooth, the little car shot through without paying, dashed against an SUV before righting itself between two lanes.

"No government is allowed to steal subconscious symbols. One phase of WILDSTYLE is conceived of a flat dimension, or paper style. This style is of the knife," he jabbed his hand against the dashboard, which was decorated like an altar to Zora Hurston, complete with red candles, fruit slices, and a chipped shot glass, "stabbing. Reality construction. Dig?"

I felt he was talking a totally different language. It sounded like English, but it wasn't no English. I looked at the little wad of money in my hand. I wondered what he intended to do with it. Would he let me keep it? "I'm sorry," I said, "I just don't understand what you're saying."

He gave a heavy sigh that sounded like a sob at first. "Knowledge knowledges knowledge." He smiled at me with tired eyes. It was like every other word he said made sense. Now, a brother in a dusty hatchback who'd just been birthed by a garbage robot suit was grilling me on some Five Percenter crypto-speak. I had to think about it.

"You're using knowledge as a verb. Knowledge not only knows but knowledge teaches knowledge. Yeah, I get it." I wasn't so stunned anymore.

"Instruments of symbolic war are: sectioners, which cut off quadrants of dimension and cause magnetic interference, and fusion of mattered space to reverse it."

Right then, the little car tipped. It actually tipped, and rolled on two wheels for what felt like five minutes. When I gathered my senses enough to open an eye to look out the window, all I saw was a blur of color and light. I tried to focus, but couldn't.

"All conceived WILDSTYLISMS do not include scenery." Ram-El looked over to me, biting his lower lip. I could see him just fine. Had he read my mind? "Iconic Treatise on Gothic Futurism: Assassins Knowledges of the Remanipulated Square Point One to 720 degrees—"

"I barely even understand what you are saying, Ram."

"Easier with suit. Heavy and hot as shit in there though."

We stopped in the Tenderloin, on Turk Street. Ram rolled the shuddering bucket in front of a five-story gray and beige building. On its side, faded paint pointed an arrow to the large cell of mailboxes guarded by an iron gate: FORT KNOX SELF STORAGE. The sign faces Hyde and Turk. Hyde is a one-way street, so none of the drivers can see the red arrow, except to maybe glimpse it from their rearview mirror as they haste through the Tenderloin shortcut.

The right side of the building receded into a stairwell filled with shadows, hemmed by a shoddy wooden fence. Plywood and barbed wire protected the kitchens and bathrooms of the residents. Secured them in their brick and dry-wall slum.

To the left, the façade smoothed out into simulated brick. Large tapering stone around the border gave way and faded. As if a giant's shoulder had rammed into the building, the painted mural that was revealed loomed over the empty fenced-in lot. Brick cast shadows on the far wall as the sun shone from inside the tenements. In the far reaches of sight, shadows of windows with no buildings and gray walls mixed in a clear blue sky.

"Got the money?" He looked at me.

"Right here." I unclenched my fist. My fingers creaked, and I noticed that I'd dug my nails into my palm. I'd been white-knuckle clutching the folded knot of money since we brushed against the Behemoth on the Bay Bridge. The top layer was damp and dark green with my sweat.

"Need some uncut diamonds."

"Right." Diamonds.

We headed across the street to a small black-and-white hand-painted sign that read, KRIM-KRAM'S PALACE OF FINE JUNK. This was Zero Group Three?

"Ram."

"Robert."

"Friend of yours?"

"Associate."

The dank and dark "palace" was about the size of an elementary school classroom, made smaller by mountains of junk—typewriters, coffee cups, VCRs, blenders, *National Geographic* magazines, antennae, remote controls, a mimeograph machine, a stack of top hats, a wall of ancient televisions, porn, lamps, nails and screws in baby food jars, picture frames, paperback books covered in mold, marbles, single socks and gloves, easels, vacuum cleaners—stacked as high as the low ceiling.

"Here's your tribute." Ram handed the man the cash.

"Not mine," Robert said as he tossed the bundle into an open drawer.

Ram walked as near to the back as he could and looked at the wall of the television sets stacked as high as the sputtering fluorescent bulb in the ceiling.

"What is this place?" I had to ask.

"People in this neighborhood can't afford your basic things. This is a brand-new secondhand store."

A black woman nearing eighty was examining a dented space heater. She checked the extension cord for frays. A five-year-old girl she was looking after flipped through a stack of ancient *Harper Brother's Weekly*s near the register. A young white guy with fresh prison tattoos had just bought one plate, one fork, one bowl, a can opener, an ashtray, and a chipped shot glass.

Robert was a thick-fingered Swede in his late fifties. His floppy gray mustache and bowl cut slumped like his gut over his belt as he soldered a wire at his workbench. "Fourth- or fifthhand, if I have anything to say about it." He examined his work.

I glanced around and didn't see Ram. He hadn't left out of the front.

"They've got us throwing away too much, way too early. They don't want us to give much adequate consideration. You know, they could stop making cars right now, and everyone in this country could get one for free every five years for the rest of their lives."

"Yeah, well, what're you gonna do?

"Plenty to do."

"What's a *krim-kram*?"

Not looking up from the jacked CD player he was tinkering with, he responded, "It's German. A *krim-kram* is like a bric-a-brac."

"A thingamajig."

"No, a thingamajig has no immediate use. A krim-kram is a piece-together."

"Like a ready-made?"

"What's a ready-made?"

"A jury-rig, a pastiche."

"Now you're just trying to confuse me."

Just then, RAM-L emerged from somewhere to my left. "Emerged" is the best way for me to describe how he just appeared. There was no lag, like I saw or heard this big-ass robot suit coming toward me.

"That's what I'm talking about," RAM said in a much clearer voice. "I seriously needed to re-up." The robot neither clanged nor hissed as he moved across the small shop heading for the front door. "Robert."

"RAM," Robert replied.

I turned to follow, but had to pause at Robert's workbench.

"Hey, man, that's no CD," I said. "That's a . . . that's a fuckin' patch . . . a rip-in . . ." Just as I'd begun to find the words, the CD was gone. Robert looked up at me as if I were crazy.

"What'd you see?" he asked, smiling at me like Captain Kangaroo.

"I saw . . . What did I see?" I found myself outside, standing next to

RAM-L about a second later, not really sure how I got there. We crossed the street, and again no one noticed.

"This suit has a device called a vokoder, it's what's letting me talk to you right now. Normally, the first thing to get twisted in our travel is language. The vokoder translates for me. But it's limited."

"I understand every word you're saying right now."

"Not really."

Passing the hatchback, we stood in the parking lot next to Fort Knox. I turned to look at the hand-written sign, KRIM-KRAM'S.

"Construction flight base is on the cipher, which flies in a spiral cipher. Included in the map and maps are conscious designs stars (misplaced dimensions), the actual firing of electromagnetic black lights (implosion), and bio-magnetic pyramids. Dimensional cracks: The travel of them will lead to other dimensions. The vokoder transmits sonic vibration variances," RAM said.

The suit began to hum like a refrigerator fritzing.

So much for the re-up, I thought, and asked, "So that was Zero Group Three?"

RAM just continued to malfunction. The humming vibrated in my stomach. The broken, intermittent pulses sounded familiar. I realized that they were notes, and that the notes were forming into a melody.

"Hey, I know that song: *Glory-glory-hallelujah / Glory-glory hallelu—hey!*"

RAM-L grabbed my arm and I fell limp as a rag doll. My instincts resisted the movement, but his strength had taken control of my arms and legs as he lifted me from the ground. He swung me toward the wall in front of us with enough force to break every bone in my face upon impact.

It's funny what you think about when you're in imminent danger. Right before the unstoppable force meets the immovable object and the truth is revealed. Right before impact, what ran through my mind was, *I should have known.*

And I should have.

All is sorrowful and rapturous.

This is an attempt to make the inaccessible accessible. To word it better, this is an attempt to have you understand things, concepts, that are around you every day and you do not see because someone has told you that they do not exist or cannot be done.

I'm talking about time travel. I'm talking about astral projection. I'm talking about perpetual motion.

Somewhere along the line, I came to believe that physical laws applied to everything. That the only realm of existence that mattered was the physical universe, and the rules I could gather from observing this universe could and should be applied at all times to all things. So now in the new millennium, it is not unusual for me to comment on certain celebrities' fall from grace by saying, "What goes up must come down." As if the law of gravity can be applied to a subject not set in a physical motion as easily as an object that has been. Now that I see it in black-and-white, does it make sense?

Perhaps this confusion of applying physical laws to the ethereal, or otherworldly, universe occurred with the secularization, or de-churchification, of our culture? Maybe I started getting my metaphors mixed up with Henry Ford assembly-line production and time-is-money Taylorism? I suspect not.

What would Heaven be like without money on Earth? Meaning, without Original Sin compounded through the debt I incur via sins as I live, anyone could get into Heaven. If a jubilee occurred, or all debts were forgiven at our demise, there would be no need for Hell, which is the most terrible debtors' prison imaginable. This celestial accounting of debits in the form of sin and credits in the form of piety, all chronicled in The Book that awaits me in my Final Audit at the Pearly Gates. Does this not sound a little too current for the Eternal All-Powerful? Does it not sound like, as you hear these words, a very commercial endeavor, possibly sponsored by Bank of America? So before time was money, my soul was money. Does that make sense?

Solid matter is solid. How's that for a law? When someone pushes you face-first into a brick wall—there's a reality you just have to accept.

When I felt the free fall of no impact—no pain or numbness of extreme pain—I flinched. I felt that something was terribly wrong and a chill ran through as relief washed over me.

"No, *this* is Zero Group Three. It's been called Zero Group Three since I first stumbled across the place, bombing the eighties."

I opened my eyes and color spun around my head. There it was, the building of black stones, rounded and the size of heads, webbed in white mortar. Above the building's several wings rose a square tower with a balcony of the same black stone. The building was little. SKOOL, the black stone sign said over the Little Black Schoolhouse. I hadn't noticed it the last time I was hear-here-here. The tower was about four stories high. The vaulted windows were paned with pebbled glass. A waist-high wall of stone went along two sides of a large informal courtyard in front of the building. I heard the rumpling metal thump of the robot suit and a clothed RAM stood beside me.

"I was here—"

"A couple of days ago. We know. That's why I was told to go back and fetch you."

"So we came in through—"

"The mural. That's right, brother. Vokoder creates frequencies that can find dimensional cracks. I can do it with a felt-tip marker too, but I'm all messed up when I Knot Frum Hear. I'm surprised you're not puking your guts out right now."

"Should I be?"

"You Knot Frum Hear?"

"Nope."

"Then, yeah, you should be a little viciously ill right now."

"Skool." The word pushed itself from my throat.

I looked back. There was nothing but water and high trees behind me. He knocked out a rhythm when we got up to the door. It creaked open to deep darkness.

"What is this place?"

"The *mundis imaginalis*, the imaginal world, on the blackhand side."

Friday

by Kenji Jasper

1.

"If my little girl's gonna smoke weed I want her to smoke it with me."

Needless to say you find her statement disturbing. With a clear mind you would most likely hit her with some raving mad rant about the problem with chickenheads and their spawn, about the piercing fear for the future that stabs you each and every time broads say something this stupid, something this honest, something this painfully poignant when thinking of the state of things on Nostrand Avenue. But you're too far gone to react in this manner.

You don't know what your watch says. But the tangerine light beyond the entrance implies that it's almost eight on a Friday in July, the Friday after the Thursday it all came apart, again. Jenna's flying the friendly skies to Rio with your downgraded replacement and you're here, having dragged your drunken self from several other heres during the course of today's binge of self-destruction.

Your cry for help began just after midday at the Star Lounge, where you were the first and only customer. Then it was on to Frank's for a few more after Mickey D's, and then here, to a closed space called Open Air, where you were summoned to say goodbye to a sister-and-a-half on her way to the Gaza Strip.

She was unsure if she would ever arrive, or make it back. But she's going because that place is her home. It's where the Palestinian blood that defines her began way back before there was the word *Palestine*, and before all of your people took that field trip across the Atlantic in shackles, surrendering themselves to New World killing fields and the mysteries at the bottom of the sea.

You savored the feeling of that sister-and-a-half's hand against your skull as she held you in a final embrace, that last shared contact before fate flung you in opposite directions; her toward home, and you to the third blood-colored couch on the left. Now you're on your third glass of amber liquid in two hours, a few chasers of ice water thrown in between. Your sister has gone on to witness the struggle of her people while you're salving the relatively superficial wounds of a love your ego ended two years ago. All that's left is this woman next to you, the one who wants to blow trees with her little girl.

"I don't want her tryin' no shit laced with crack," she continues earnestly, having already confessed that it takes a whole week for her to burn through a full spliff. She works in publishing to pay the bills while she dreams of making stylish threads for folks like herself.

You can't fully place the exact moment she joined you. Perhaps it was after you complimented her on the head of curled braids coming out of her scalp and the shades that looked designer without the price tag. Or maybe it was she who spoke first. Either way the two of you are now together, now acting as one in the ancient art of bullshit conversation.

"She's five," the mother informs me. "I was only twenty when I had her."

The big two-zero. The end of innocence and the start of ignorance. The decade of false starts and delusions of grandeur rolling into the biggest dildo of your lifetime. You have to smile in remembering who you were back then, that church boy who only wanted to make his mama happy, your hair brushed forward until your scalp was raw so you could get those waves.

The big two-zero. You were dead in the center of college and that big-tittied girl with the devilish smile had promised you the world with a side of stars. It was you who pushed her into that fling she had. Then she pushed you out the door for being everything he wasn't. Ten years later you're still picking up the pieces, still moping through tears you didn't cry, for a train to the promised land that never left the station. Jenna was your second chance, and you blew it.

"I feel old," she says of being a ripe twenty-five, before she drains her latest glass of J.D. and something else.

Her eyes wear that glaze of tipsiness. But it'll take at least two more to get her full-blown drunk. Ready. Set. Go.

"You wanna come outside with me and smoke?" she asks politely, her firm thigh now brushing against your own. As she stands you get the first good look at her. Five feet, three inches, maybe a B-cup, with flesh of honey-brown and ample junk in the trunk. First-generation Haitian-American with dreams bigger than her booty.

She's the kind of girl you prayed for back in the early years, when the Mount Gay and Cokes were all that could numb you from the repeated blows of the same party night after night. You prayed for someone to come and tell you her dreams, to make you a meal that wouldn't be served in Styrofoam or out of a box, a perfect thigh to rest your head on when the check you needed did not arrive.

You would've done anything for that: massaged every inch of her being, and put your lips to her shrine until your neck went sore. You would've blown your next three checks before they even cleared on whatever she wanted for that kind of simple girlfriend bullshit.

Unfortunately your prayers were not answered then. It took two years and a twelve-block move before Jenna came along, speaking Kingston patois or the King's English, depending on who was around, and convincing you that there wasn't a more beautiful soul in all of Brooklyn. But by then ego had already taken hold. By then that up-and-coming rapper had sent Ms. X to your room with an iced bottle of Verve and nothing else, just to make sure the cover story came out right. By then you burned a J every forty-eight hours and thought like a criminal. And of course that all came out in the wash while she was on dry detail. That's what the liquor's for now, to get you wet again.

"I keep setting the date and then pushing it back," she says after a puff from her Salem. Your Newport burns more quickly. Maybe it's the alleged cleaning fluid in the ingredients.

Her baby daddy's made it big out in La-La Land and wants to pick up the tab for a two-parent family, a recipe for bliss equipped with a white picket fence and a platinum Visa. Of course she doesn't want it. Because she doesn't love him anymore. And at twenty-five, midway through a decade of ignorance, love is all that matters.

The voice in your head seconds the motion. Here she is, a struggling single mom crammed into a matchbook of an apartment on a pittance of a paycheck, and there's a Prince Charming offering up deliverance on a platter, a free merge into the express lane to happiness and security squared. This is the kind of shit that only happens on UPN or in the pages of the lamest brand of black fiction, and yet she's willing to toss it over the side for nothing more than lovey-dovey emotion. She's young and stupid, and you, at this point, are definitely drunk off your ass.

"Love is overrated, honey," you assure her with slurred speech, your intonation making the words arrive like a balled fist.

"What's that supposed to mean?" she rebuts before a hard pull on her square.

"Just what it says," you reply. "Love ain't pertinent to your survival."

"Well, I think it is," she shoves back, now fully charged with aggravation. "I think it's more important than anything else when you're trying to choose your partner for life. I don't know about you but for me that's just some shit I gotta have."

You retreat a step backward. The muscles have flexed in her left quad. Her arm is bent at a perfect right angle as her hand rests on the curve of her right hip.

"Maybe I've just lived a different life," you utter. "Maybe I just chose people that made love hard, or maybe loving *me* is hard."

Now you've definitely blown it. Any edge you might have had has been filed smooth. That façade of cool indifference has gone the way of sweaters with leather patches and Troop gym shoes. Now she can see your pain. Now she can put her finger through that hole where your heart was on the Thursday before this Friday, when hope was a volume of empty words recited for the millionth time.

You await your dismissal. You expect her to suck her teeth and sashay down the block toward the closest neo-soul-lovin' nigga in vintage disco gear. You've already prepared the *Fuck you, bitch!* that will be needed to maintain your New York rep as an asshole.

But she does not leave. As a matter of fact she doesn't move at all. Her eyes compromise what's left of the shield you made certain no broad would ever breach. And you don't even know her name.

"She isn't all of us, you know." Her verbal assault continues, evaporating the last of the pimp juice in your veins.

"I know," you spill dejectedly. "But she was the one."

"And he's *not* the one for me, you see what I mean?"

You do but you won't admit that you do. Because if you confess to the black male sin of self-awareness, if you stand here and fully admit to the next girl you'd like to fuck that you hate yourself for betraying the truest love you could ever have possibly conceived, then that would be growing up. And even now, at thirty-four, you still ain't ready to do that shit.

"I see what you sayin' and all," you reply, glazing the words with fake conceit. "I mean, *you* got a tough decision to make."

She knows that she has you, even if she doesn't particularly want you. But the positioning is there. Her troops outnumber yours three to one. Yet she's playing it cool. And you're even cooler, the both of you waiting to see which move the next piece will make.

"Why is it that we never get it how we want it?" she asks, sucking her Salem down to nothing, as if you should know just because you're nine years older.

"Because we'd find something wrong with it," you say with a clarity that surprises even you. "Because if we got what we wanted we'd never have anything to dream about."

Her features freeze, a page taking too long to load. Something tells you the tables are turning.

"What are you thinking?" you ask.

"About Brooklyn," she says.

"What about it?" you follow up. She's on the ropes. One more shot and she's spread-eagle on your queen-size Posturepedic with the freshly changed maroon sheets.

"Your house," she grins. Maybe you told her you owned it. Maybe that impressed her enough to donate her panties ahead of schedule. "I wanna see it."

You smile wide. She is yours, at least until morning.

"But not tonight," she continues.

ᘒ

The two of you abandon Open Air for The Bitter End. Along the way you pull a daisy from someone's flowerbed and she puts it between her braids like a coffeehouse Billie Holiday (sans the H problem). She giggles like a five-year-old. You grin like a dirty old man.

A woman of the darkest brown is at the mic giving her soul to a song called "Whispers." The sign out front says her name is Chanda. You'd buy the record if there was one.

"So, did you go to college?" she inquires. This is the question you hate answering, mainly due to the embarrassment factor that usually accompanies it. The believability of the experience diminishes with every year you age. The debutantes and gold diggers, the feminist zealots and vegan enthusiasts, the jocks on the football team who were always a joke, and a thousand hours of lectures and losers who thought graduating from a "school of distinction" made them special.

You finished at the top of your class. A nice enterprising young man once deemed a history maker of tomorrow. Go figure.

"Yeah," you say.

"Well, I didn't. Always wish I had though."

"You got time," you tell her.

"It doesn't seem like it."

"But you do. You're just getting to the point where you understand *you*. Next thing you gotta figure is what you want. If school is a part of that then you'll go and get the piece of paper. You'll get whatever you need."

Sobriety arrives and brings the scene into focus: the basket of fried calamari and glasses of ice water, the pleather booth at a perfect distance from the stage, the trio of Asian girls across the way in short skirts with legs to die for. The clock over the bar reads ten-thirty.

"You think so?" she asks.

"Yeah, I do," you say with an assuring grin.

She glances over at the clock. "Damn, how long have we been here?"

"Long enough," you say.

She has to go. You walk her to the F and tell her how to get to the A. It won't take her long. The trains are still running express. You don't want her to go. You don't want her to leave you amidst all of this temptation, all of these potholed roads that lead nowhere. But you'd never tell her that, not even if you had a week to live, 'cause that's more evolution than you're ready for.

She writes her number on the back of your card, which she does not take, and gives you a smile before descending into the world below. You watch her until she is no more, wondering if you'll ever see her again. But all thoughts stop when you get that empty feeling in the pit of you, that pain of knowing that you're all alone.

You can't deal with that shit now, not with everything that's just happened. You can't go home. You can't go back to Nostrand Ave., where they all know you and yet treat you like a stranger. You flip open your cell and dial the number for the magic man, who just happens to be home this late on a Friday. The time has come to escape again. You hail a cab for Harlem.

2.

"I hear shit is mad hot down in the BK," my dealer says, as he packs my purchase in a plastic bag of the richest blue. The lit L in hand is a complimentary bonus burn.

From the words and the given situation the average sucker might assume my dealer to be some reggaed-out Jamaican with a natty beard, locks, and a multicolored crown. Yet the truth is, he's a blond, green-eyed gay boy from Scarsdale with three grad degrees and no legitimate job to speak of.

Josh was a dissertation away from being a doctor of Linguistics when his Z3 had a head-on collision with an MTA bus. He lived and the bus driver and three other people died under circumstances stranger than your fiction, walking away from what was left of his car with nothing more than a concussion and a fractured clavicle. After that, life was too short, and dissertations take too fucking long anyway.

He came home, packed up a suitcase of all the shit that mattered, and walked out of his East Side condo never to return again. Three months later he sold the place for a million and bought his way into a co-op of hydro growers in South Florida. Needless to say his bags are never bad, and he can hold a good convo longer than either of your dealers back around the way.

"Whachu mean?" you ask, pretending that you don't know what he knows you know.

"Jamaicans blowing up buildings with nitro. Some cop gets popped with a banger somebody stole from his squad car the day before."

"Don't believe everything you hear," you say, as he makes the eye of the L glow red.

"I don't. That was in the paper today." Amidst all the drinking you forgot to grab the *Daily News*.

"Are you for real?" you ask.

"I'd show it to you myself if I hadn't left my paper at Veg City this morning."

"Veg City. Yeah, I forgot you're on that vegan shit."

"I keep telling you: It'll add thirty years to your life."

"I'll take a closed casket," you say with a grin.

"Watch what you say," he replies. "That wouldn't make your mother happy."

"She'll probably be the one that pulls the trigger," you fire back, anticipating the soon-to-arrive moment when the high will kick in, when that tingling sensation will travel the length of your limbs and soft palms massage your hypothalamus.

But that moment has yet to arrive. Instead your concentration targets the flat plasma screen displaying the latest in balladic music video: a man and woman sealed in a room; his hand to her bare ankle; his tongue to a perfect set of toes; water cascading down half-naked bodies shaped and toned by too many hours at the local weight pile.

The imagery is more than familiar. But in your version the girl is Jenna. And Jenna's darker than the girl on the screen. The crease in Jenna's spine is closer to perfect as it channels into and through the junk in her trunk.

You think of the mornings after all those nights when the two of you went for bonus rounds between scrubs and rinses. Your palms were the perfect clasp for the heart shape of her behind. You remember the dangerous feeling that she was about to slip through your hands onto cast iron and porcelain that could've killed her. So you held tighter, you made each thrust more fluid, grinding your heels into the bathmat, feeling the way she became you, that way you dissolved into her great space of being.

These thoughts give you the worst erection, the kind of thing you'd like to avoid in front of the gay white boy in fear that he might infer certain things that just aren't true. Still, you can't help thirsting for the fluid that once flowed freely from within her. No, you *thirst* for her. But *he's* probably sucking that well dry as you merely fantasize, seated in a twenty-first-century opium den, teetering on the verge of whacking off in front of the fag weed dealer who's trying to tell you that crucial moves are being made on Nostrand Avenue. He could even be telling you that your life is in danger. But the beginnings of your high are making reception far less than transparent.

"You got an out if shit gets hot?" he poses after retrieving the blunt.

To be truthful, the very idea of this sounds excessive. An out? It's not like you just jacked the local supplier for a few dozen kilos, or hit some high-line fence for his take on some big score. You just draw blueprints. You make plans. You combine journalism and fiction to give folks an idea of how to pull off a perfect heist, and then you walk away. So why would you ever have to leave Nostrand Avenue? The very idea of it sounds ridiculous.

"Yeah, if I got to," you say in a more arrogant manner than even you thought was possible.

"And you got heat too, right?" You nod, this time lying completely through your teeth.

"Fine," he says. "Then you're good to go."

You wonder how much he really knows about what you've done. And then you ask yourself to whose benefit might your answers serve. Why are you letting him know so much when he's told you so little? Are you really this gullible? Are thugs about to storm the apartment armed with silenced .45s and more unpleasant means to make you talk? Or could you just be high and paranoid?

You do the cash-for-bag exchange and get the fuck outta there, glancing over your shoulder as you run all the way down to the street. Next thing you know you're at the corner of One Hundred Twenty-fifth and Amsterdam. One o'clock is kissing two. And you still don't want to go home.

You wish you could just stay in the streets and be one with the nature of what New York used to be: scope-out kids doing pieces on bodega walls, black writers reading from books that actually mattered in venues open twenty-four/seven, Spanish girls with perfect hips and tits that say *papi* all the time and love them some Negroes. Why can't that New York be *your* New York?

You unholster your cell in hopes of scoring an easy piece of tail, only to end up talking to a whole bunch of voice greetings. You don't leave any messages but you do flag a cab to City Hall.

On the way down you revel in the heights of your "elevation." There's an added gleam to brake lights and turn signals, horns and screeches. Giggles and screams are all amplified tenfold. You're reminded of those Michelob commercials you used to love, with all those young yuppies dressed up real slick in downtown New York. You never wondered where the black people were. But at twelve, those scenes had been way too cool for you to even want to ask questions.

There's a vision of teenage love at the park off the West Side Highway. A silhouette of boy and girl locking lips to the syncopated flow of the Hudson. A cigarette is plucked from the window of an Eclipse to bounce off your cabdriver's windshield. He curses in a language you can't even describe.

You close your eyes to just feel the sensation provided by the THC. This is your life, a spinning, hollow-tipped projectile aimed at nothing in particular. You could have been delivered a million times: the associate editor gig in Chicago, the language arts teacher thing out in Trenton, or even church on just the right Sunday. You promised Jenna you would never binge like this again. Actually, you promised each other.

She was as bad as you. Weed, liquor, and two packs of Parliaments a day. Sometimes coke, sometimes X. Braid a few rappers' girlfriends and you get access to everything. But then her father died, and you guess she decided to stop fighting being herself. With the man she was just like gone, she decided to take his place.

She wanted you to quit too. She wanted you to write more than a page a day. She wanted you to be who you were supposed to be. And you hated her for it.

Six months later you were at that bar on Fourth Avenue, a Jewish hand on one thigh, a Cuban tongue in your left ear. Wannabe Paris Hilton broads without the dough or endorsement deals. It was too easy, except with all the rum and smoke and ego you forgot you'd given Jenna those keys. It escaped you that she said she might come through after work. And plus, the devil in you was like, *Fuck her and her goody-two-shoes bullshit!* You were gonna do you. And you're still doing it, riding downtown in a yellow cab on some useless Sade "Is It a Crime" music-video bullshit.

The cab stops right in front of the Brooklyn Bridge. You peel off a fifty and make your driver's day. Then it's time to walk the plank.

You've strolled the Brooklyn Bridge twice before, but were never this blown or depressed. It won't surprise you if you decide to do a Louganis over the side and land right between the jaws of the Creature from the Black Lagoon. And you'd be equally nonchalant about collapsing before you got to the other end.

Yet you know you'll make it, because you always do, because there's something about you that ensures your survival no matter how much damage you inflict on yourself. You know you're better than this. Maybe someday you'll actually realize it.

Lives streak by beneath you in both directions, each soul symbolized by a pair of low beams. You wonder where they're going and what they'll do there. You miss that car you wrecked and the bike that got stolen. You miss not having to wait for some other guy to take you home and then charge you for it. But those days are as gone as she is and there's nothing you can do about it.

Forty minutes later you find your way to a B26 with your name on it. Joined only by a mother of two and a four-hundred-pound security guard eating White Castles, you're back on Nostrand Avenue in fifteen minutes. Turning onto the block, you see that line of light at the bottom of the horizon. Friday's finished. The next question is whether you'll even be alive for Saturday.

Love, Rage, and Volkswagens

by SékouWrites

I remember when I bought my first car . . .
  A Volkswagen Rabbit I bought from my next door neighbor for a hundred bucks
    Couldn't even drive it yet cuz the CV joint was broken—
    (whatever that was)
    but it didn't matter cuz it was mine
    so I sat inside of it anyway
    content to dream of future dayz
    Then, it happened . . .

John Elliot Square sits at the top of a hill in the Roxbury section of Boston. When I was young, it was decorated mostly by shards of broken liquor bottles. I moved away after the fourth grade and every time I came back to visit my father, the square looked a little better. It was many years before I understood that my father's not-for-profit organization was responsible for these incremental but profound changes.

One summer, I returned to find that my father had relocated from the brownstone I grew up in to the middle of John Elliot Square, right across the street from a massive white church that has always been the area's focal point. His new residence was a corner penthouse in a building that his Roxbury Action Program had transformed from an empty shell with vacant windows into a posh apartment complex of citywide renown.

That summer was also the first time in my life that I was earning real money. My father had set me up with one of his friends in construction and I was working to the very pleasant tune of nine hundred dollars a week— more than a grand with overtime. There was hardly enough time to spend part of the first check before the next one was being counted out in crisp fifty-dollar bills. I felt grown. Independent. But one thing was missing. The Holy Grail of teenage status symbols: a car.

Behind my father's new place, there was a wide parking lot and a grassy field that rolled downhill, almost to the steps of the house next door, a yellow and white two-story. Similar in design to my father's complex, it had a wide strip of gravel behind it that served as a parking lot for residents. Every day the parking area remained empty except for a white Volkswagen Rabbit that never moved.

After a long workday of having to ride with strangers from one construction job to another, I rang the doorbell of the yellow house on a whim and asked the man who answered the door if he might be interested in selling the Volkswagen.

While he and his roommate made tea, they explained that the engine ran, but the car couldn't be driven because the CV joint was broken. This being my first car-buying experience, I had no idea what a CV joint might be, but since I was making more money than I knew what to do with, I wasn't very concerned about how much it would cost to repair. Plus, as a young man anxious to undertake the next crucial step toward adulthood, I didn't want to appear amateurish by asking what a CV joint was, so I just nodded in a way that I hoped would come off as nonchalant. They looked at each other, shrugged, and said if I wanted it I could have it for a hundred bucks. Before they could change their minds, I peeled off two fifties and took the keys with a smile.

I couldn't wait to get off work the next day. As soon as I got home, I went next door to sit in my new car, get a feel for it, see if there was anything else that needed to be fixed, and enjoy the feeling of having made my very first grownup purchase. I'd already placed the requisite auto-body calls, and it was only going to cost me two hundred dollars to fix the constant velocity joint—including the tow to the shop—so I was more than a little pleased with myself for finagling a meager three-hundred-dollar admission into the world of mobile independence.

Still parked behind the yellow house, the Volkswagen looked exactly the same. Except it was mine. That fact alone made it seem to glow. When

I turned the key for the first time, the engine purred at me while I tinkered with the stereo and diddled with the stick shift. *My own car*, I thought, smiling at myself in the rearview mirror. Mission accomplished. I was still tuning the radio presets when I heard the first shout.

> *I saw the gun before I saw the billy club*
> *I saw the billy club before I saw the badge*
> *and all I could think was*
> *I'm glad I'm not already dead*
> *I'm nineteen*
> *and only twenty seconds ago*
> *I was floating on cloud nine*
> *whiling away the meantime*
> *thinking about how blessed I am*
> *to finally be buying something of mine*
> *but now . . .*
> *now, it's three of them*
> *versus one of me*
> *and I don't know which way to turn*
> *or what to do*
> *becuz it's three of them*
> *versus one of me*
> *and I don't know how the hell to raise the flag*
> *that tells these boyzinblue*
> *I'm not the nogoodnigga they mistook me for*
> *I'm not a nigga at all*
> *I'm just . . . me*

I was shocked that it was even possible for anyone to mistake me for a criminal. As a bright college student at Morehouse, I'd had many philosophic conversations about racism, mostly as an abstract and distant idea.

I'd discussed the media's perpetuation of a standard of beauty that did not include the physical dimensions of full-figured black women. I'd revisited the meaning of many major holidays and reëxamined them from a more Afrocentric perspective. I'd given an amateur speech chastising African-Americans for using racism as an excuse to underachieve and been dealt a swift and powerful lesson about institutionalized racism in response. I was learning to redefine myself as a self-aware black man in a society that does not always have our best interests at heart. I was learning. Growing. Knowing. But nowhere in those late-night talks and lunchroom debates had anyone raised the issue of personal racism. None of us had told each other stories of being victimized by police or the powers that be. None of us had talked about being forced into a police lineup or beaten like Rodney King.

And in the underlying subtext, I suppose, many of us felt that we weren't destined for that type of disrespect. That we, the good seeds, "the talented tenth," had less to worry about from the law. It was our brothers and sisters out on the block doing dirt and chasing sin who had to fear that up-close-and-personal type of racism. Not us. Not the African-American sons of doctors, lawyers, and civil rights leaders. Not the sons of parents who told us that because of their struggles we wouldn't have to endure the same hardships. That pain was for their generation, our parents told us. Not for ours. Then again, maybe we never talked about personal racism at school because the experiences that pain us the most are usually the ones we are least willing to share.

No matter the reason, when three white officers approached me with batons drawn and derision in their voices, I had no frame of reference. No internal dialogue. No easily recallable experience or anecdote to help me through.

I remember the hot shame of standing in the middle of the neighborhood that my father had recreated, certain that friends and admirers of his were seeing me surrounded by police. I remember the anger. The burn of indignation that flared so brightly, so suddenly, that only my fear of retaliation kept it at bay.

Then, when they scream at me to put my hands on the hood of my own car
it dawns on me that maybe I need to be that other kind of nogoodnigga
That take no shit kind of nogoodnigga

That "fuck your badge
and your gun
shoot me now
or get your sergeant on the phone" kind of nogoodnigga
Why didn't my mother tell me that there would be dayz
when I might have to be that kind of nogoodnigga?
So I make my decision
I grit my teeth
& I refuse to turn around
refusing to put my hands on the hood of my own car
on my block
next to my father's house
for sitting in the car
that I just paid for
with my own money . . .
Oh, no. Not today
I turn into that kind of nogoodnigga
silent, but deadly . . .

I felt the danger. I knew I was seconds away from certain pain and possible death, but there was something inside me that shifted as I stood there. I felt a defiance come over me. A quiet conviction that if it was to happen this way, at least I would have kept my dignity by refusing to be treated as a common criminal. In that moment next to my Volkswagen, I found an unexpected reservoir of strength.

And I won't turn around
so they speak louder
and I will not turn around
so they yell louder
and I still will not turn around
so they scream louder
I see the billy clubs come up
and I know this, right here,

right now
is my last chance
so I start to turn
and then I'm like—hell, no
I cross my arms
and lean against the fender
with a look that says "you do what you gotta do" in my eyes
even though the corners are stinging
but I'm not gonna cry
not here, not now, not today
and I'm not gonna fuckin' turn around either
so if you got something for me, officer
then let me see it coming
The billy clubs start to fall
and I brace for impact
and then one of them looks at my chest . . . and stops . . . and asks
"You in school?"
I look down to see my Morehouse College sweater
blazing out as my current non-nogoodnigga sign

Seconds away from the beating of my life and it's my dingy Morehouse sweatshirt that saves me? With the famous police powers of perception it took something as obvious as a college sweater to alert them to the fact that I was not a common thug? What about my speech patterns? My Polo framed glasses? My expensive jewelry, without the slightest hint of bling? At the same time, in the same moment, I was happy I had worn that sweatshirt simply for what might have happened to me if I hadn't.

I nodded at them in response and they demanded my college ID. It was difficult to maintain my composure. Harder still when they sent me up to the house like an errand boy to fetch the sellers of the car and thereby prove my claim of being the new owner. With each passing second, each indignity layered on top of the last, I found myself wanting to scream at them. To tell them that enough was enough. But these thoughts were tempered by my fear of what might happen if I did.

At the front door, I knocked and rang the bell like a man possessed, driven by fear and the urge to vindicate myself, but no one was home. As I leaned against the front door feeling defeated, I realized I was out of the police officers' line of direct sight and I thought seriously about running the other way.

Deciding not to flee was one of the hardest things I've done, but I forced myself to return to the backyard with my story uncorroborated. I expected the worst but to my surprise the mood had shifted. Correction, their mood had shifted. While I was just as angry and embarrassed and fearful as ever, they were suddenly relaxed and conversational.

They tried to joke me into a better mood and engage me in idle chatter about the merits of Volkswagens. I wasn't amused. I kept my arms crossed, my mouth closed, my eyes locked into the distance.

and I'm happy that I'm not lying on the ground bleeding
with three feet in my behind
but I feel guilty about that joy
cuz what if I hadn't had that sweatshirt on?
Or what if I had turned my back like they told me to?
Or what if I was one of those brothers on the block who didn't have a college
   sweatshirt to put on
but yet and still I was not a nogoodnigga?
What about then?
So I listen through the apology
about how some good Samaritan neighbor called it in
And I ask what for
And they say
"Stripping the car"
And I wanna say
"How the hell am I gonna strip a car from the inside?"
but I don't
cuz then they might figger
I know too much about the ways of a nogoodnigga
and take me in anyway

So instead I walk away
Intact
Not bleeding
But I'm mad as hell
& my eyes are still stinging
And I'm thinking
about how
on some days
in some ways
maybe it does pay
to be that other kind of nogoodnigga
Not the kind that's no good to me
or no good to my family
or no good to women
or no good to my people
but the kind of nogoodnigga that ain't no good at all . . .
to them.

I kept my composure until I was twenty yards away. Far enough that I hoped they couldn't see my shoulders begin to sag and the first tear finally make its way onto my cheek.

I spent the rest of the day staring out at the city from the patio surrounding my father's penthouse and thinking about how my life of relative privilege hadn't afforded me a bit of difference in the eyes of those beyond my community. When my father came home and asked me what was wrong, I said "nothing" and it passed in that uncomfortable way that fathers and sons shield each other from their pain.

August 2003. Summer again, so many years after buying that hundred-dollar Volkswagen. I finally told my father, my mother, and about sixty strangers what happened to me that summer day. They were sitting in the audience while I performed my part of a spoken-word performance play during the New York International Fringe Festival. The performance addressed the everyday realities of being a black man in modern

America, and during the show I recited a poem about buying the Volkswagen.

After the performance, we went out to dinner at a restaurant next door to the playhouse. My parents were proud and full of smiles about their son, the writer, who had just made the leap to writer-slash-off-Broadway-performer, but every once in a while I would catch them staring into places far beyond our dining table.

"Hey, Mom," I called, attempting to break one of her pensive reveries with some levity. "You can't sigh so loudly during the show. It almost threw me off."

Instantly, she was leaning toward me, flickers of subdued rage sparking to life behind her glasses.

"Well, I wouldn't be sighing if I hadn't been finding out all these horrible stories about my son." Before I could reply, she was already turning to my father, and for the first time I noticed that despite many years of divorce, Mom and Dad were seated together, united in their son's pain.

"Did he tell you?" she asked my father. He glanced down, his smile and good cheer fading momentarily. If I hadn't been staring at him I would have certainly missed the small motion that passed for him shaking his head, no.

"But I saw it in Boston," he said, referring to the fundraiser we'd held prior to the show's New York opening. I smiled then, remembering that right in the middle of our fundraiser performance, just after I'd recited the Volkswagen poem, my father had stood up, walked onstage, and hugged me powerfully. It wasn't until he sat back down that we could continue the show.

He and I never talked about that moment or the incident that originally inspired the poem, but when I purchased the Volkswagen, I felt like I had taken a step toward adulthood. Yet when that rite of passage was superceded by another, more painful one, I learned that for black men in America, the sting of personal racism is the unfortunate rite of passage that many of us find shaping our lives, personalities, and destinies. And my father's hug was my congratulations for surviving.

Marine Tiger

by Jerry A. Rodriguez

Some of my fondest childhood memories are of early Saturday mornings when I would be awakened by my father's singing: satin soundwaves of passion flooding every room as he crooned along to the sensually charged Latin boleros he adored so unequivocally.

I'd lay in bed, soft cotton sheet tucked under my chin, vision still slightly blurred—my ears filled with the clamor of violins wailing for a lost lover, percussion palpitating like a parade of broken hearts, horns pleading for the excruciating longing to end in the poetically romantic ballads which were the soundtrack of my father's youth. Those long-gone days when as a teenager he'd spend every afternoon sitting on the porch of his family's lopsided wooden house in Santurce, sipping sweet black coffee, waiting to see my mother come strutting down the dirt road; verdant hills and vast blue skies looming behind her as she made her way back from school many miles away.

Barefoot, wearing faded flower-print dresses, books and shoes clutched to her luxuriant bust, head shyly bowed, Mami would nervously glance at Pop through locks of curly black hair. She was his brown skin vision, *una trigueña bien chévere* with wide hips, dark piercing Taino Indian eyes, a noble Moorish nose, and sensuous African lips all wrapped in smooth skin the color of cinnamon. My father would strum his *guitarra* and fervently serenade her with many of the same songs he'd continue singing during their fifty years of marriage together.

Pop could always rely on the music to take him back. After a week of hard work building kitchen cabinets with hands, sweat, hammer, nails, and saw, Saturday mornings were his special time. Pop would sink into his plush easy chair, eyes closed, head tilted back, listening to his collection of scratchy old records. He was a compact man with a voice grander than life.

A voice as lush and passionate as the great crooners he derived such immense pleasure from: Santos Colón, Roberto Ledesma, Tito Rodríguez, and Daniel Santos. Singers he eagerly accompanied every weekend, their voices transporting him back to *la isla*, to the sparkling turquoise ocean, the heaven-kissing palm trees, the melodious song of the *coquí* floating on tropical breezes. An enchanted place very far away from the dirty, depressing concrete streets of *Nueva Jork*.

Everyone in our Brooklyn neighborhood knew my father well. They admired him, respected him. Some even feared him. Everyone either called him by the nickname Paquito or Don Paco. Though he was a congenial, generous man—who without a second thought helped and advised all who asked—he was also hard-boiled and hot-tempered enough to keep the street gangs and stickup kids from coming around our block. One thing Pop never tolerated was anyone who preyed on the weak and helpless. If he hadn't been such a devoted family man, he would've made a hell of a gangster, just like his own father.

When Mom and Pop arrived in New York during the late forties, they took the same route many other Puerto Ricans did at that time. They traveled across the Atlantic crammed on a huge steamship christened *The Marine Tiger* and ended up in that faraway land called El Bronx. For the first few weeks they were taunted as they strolled down the street. Groups of brawny Italian men standing on street corners would shout, "Marine Tiger! Go home Marine Tiger!" Though my mother would get offended and become upset, my father shrugged it off. He didn't care what they thought. He was in the big city and was going to make a life for himself and the children they would one day have.

Since my father was such a diminutive man in contrast to other kids' fathers, I never thought of him as much of a tough guy. He was about five-six, with a potbelly and rippling arms, his shiny, ebony hair slicked back with pomade, a perfectly clipped mustache showcasing a charming and irresistible smile that made the edges of his friendly brown eyes crinkle.

Though I knew how hard he was on my older brother Flaco, who was always getting into trouble and incurring Pop's wrath, I never feared my father. I guess since I was much younger and a fairly introverted kid, I didn't get a genuine ass-whoopin' until I was a bit older and more rebellious. The side of my father I knew back in the day was that of a big-hearted, gentle man. A man with a generous grin who with much enthusiasm built me elaborate wooden toys like swords, shields, and stilts, and always made me laugh with a quick joke, a tickle, and a wink of the eye. But I discovered a very different side of him back in 1969 when I was eight.

Our next door neighbor Milagros Gonzalez was my first crush. She was a hot twenty-six-year-old with shapely legs, a to-die-for ass, and breasts perfect as papayas. Her wavy auburn hair came down to her waist and she always wore tight, revealing dresses, which kept a steady stream of drooling suitors knocking on her door.

A sweet, hard-working girl, Milagros seemed to somehow attract the worst kind of men. Guys Mami called *títeres*. I always heard yelling, the sounds of doors slamming and glass breaking coming from her apartment, a testament to the many nasty domestic squabbles she'd have with her boyfriends.

I would often stay up late at night reading comic books while hidden under a tent of sheets, clutching a flashlight. My mother disapproved of me reading so many comics and wanted me to devote more of my time to reading books.

She would say, "Daniel Ocasio! Why are you always reading that junk? When I was in fifth grade in Puerto Rico, we were reading *Les Misérables* and *Don Quixote*. Literature! That's what makes you smart. Not those funny books you love so much!" She was right, of course, and I did read plenty of novels, but I loved comics more and dreamed of one day becoming an artist.

Since I can remember, I've been drawing superheroes, villains, and worlds of fantasy; which is how I make a living these days, and my folks are very proud of my career as an illustrator. But when I was kid, so as not to aggravate Mami too much, I'd read *Fantastic Four*, *Daredevil*, and *The Amazing Spider-Man* on the sneak, losing myself in the art of Jack Kirby and Steve Ditko, and my imagination would soar.

One night, as I was drawing the Silver Surfer, I heard a car screech to a halt. My curious nature got the better of me so I climbed out of bed, tiptoed across the squeaky floor, and peeked out of my second-floor window. There was a dilapidated green Impala parked in front of the empty garbage-strewn lot across the street, its noisy, drooping muffler belching clouds of black smoke into the steamy summer night. I knew the jalopy well; it belonged to Ray, Milagros's latest loser boyfriend. I grabbed my 007 binoculars off the dresser to get a better view.

Milagros was inside the car having a heated argument. Within moments they were screaming at the top of their lungs. I glanced over at Flaco, asleep in a tangle of wrinkled sheets. (I was always amazed that neighborhood kids could set off fireworks outside our window and my brother would remain like the dead man at a wake; nothing and no one could disturb him.) I looked back outside, just in time to see Milagros give Ray a vigorous shove to the chest. I flinched and held my breath when he returned the favor with a wicked backhand slap across her mouth, splitting her bottom lip. I was suddenly filled with rage and wished I was Spider-Man, so I could swing down to the shadow-washed street, beat the hell out of the villainous Ray, and save the beautiful girl.

Ray grabbed Milagros by her slender wrists. She feverishly struggled to break free but he was way too strong. She finally calmed down, and as soon as he let go of her, she bolted from the car and screamed.

"I hate you!"

In a drunken stupor, Ray stumbled out of the Impala and almost fell. His white Panama hat and burgundy polyester suit made him look like a cheap hood from Hell's Kitchen. I could barely see his reptilian face in the darkness but I knew he was a hard, scary-looking man, with stone-cold eyes and a nasty scar running across his jaw. Ray stood swaying in the middle of the silent, desolate street. For a moment he seemed unsure of where he was, or what he intended to do. He abruptly began to scream a litany of obscenities.

"*Puuttaaa*! You little cunt. Get your ass back here before I kill you, *canto de cabróna sucia!*"

Ray's rum-infused ranting awoke my mother, who immediately became unhinged. She narrowed her stern eyes and roughly shook my father by the shoulder.

"Paco! *Levantaté!* Wake up."

Pop sat up, let out a yawn, and in a raspy voice asked, "What's wrong, *negra?*"

"Listen to that filth," Mami replied as Ray continued to scream and curse. "That's *el títere ese*. Milagros's boyfriend."

"Again?" My father struggled his way out of bed, went to the window, and shouted, "Hey, *mira*! People are trying to sleep. *Cállate la boca!*"

Ray scowled at my father and gave him the finger. "Fuck you!"

Pop turned to Mami, who sat in bed, arms folded across her chest, the elaborate ruffled collar of her sheer pink nightgown framing her angry face. Though Mom was in her forties, Pop thought she still looked as beautiful as she did the first time he set eyes on her back in Puerto Rico. But he was quite disturbed by the way she was glaring at him, like Ray's screaming was *his* fault. Ray continued his vocal barrage, so Pop marched out of the bedroom determined to shut the man up.

I feigned sleep as he opened the door to my room and the jarring light from the hallway spilled in. Pop went to Flaco's bed, poking and prodding my big brother out of his coma. Peeking from under the sheet I stared at my father, who was wearing only a big pair of yellow boxers and nothing else. Scrutinizing his muscular arms, round belly, and thin, hairless legs, I wondered how he would fare in battle against someone like Ray, a foot taller and sixty pounds heavier. Flaco finally woke up, trying to rub the sleep from his eyes.

"Whaa? It's morning already?"

"No. But we have to go outside and take care of a problem. Get up."

In a daze, Flaco slipped into blue jeans and dirty hi-top Converses. Flaco was fifteen, exceptionally tall, and skinny as a broomstick. His head was covered with a stocking and he could barely keep his brooding, heavy-lidded eyes open as he dutifully followed my father out the room.

I immediately jumped out of bed and dashed to the window, my heart pounding in excitement as I looked through the binoculars. Pop confidently swaggered to the middle of the street wearing nothing but his underwear, followed by Flaco, who continued rubbing his eyes, staggering like a zombie who had just crawled out of the grave. My brother was a tough kid but I wondered how much help he was going to be to Pop, since he was obviously out of it. I was terrified they would both end up badly hurt. Ray became quiet and looked my father up and down as if he was an escapee from a mental institution.

"What the hell you want, ah?" Ray asked, his eyes filled with belligerence.

In his heavy Spanish accent, my father spoke deliberately and evenly, like Ray was slightly retarded or something.

"It's one in the morning. I have to go to work at sunrise. My sons have to go to school. And your filthy mouth has made my wife very upset. I do not like my family hearing such language."

Ray cackled as if this was the funniest thing he'd ever heard. "Are you kiddin' me? Little Man and Punk Son supposed to scare me?"

"You are trying my patience."

"So? What the fuck you gonna do, *cabrón*?" Ray reached into his jacket pocket and whipped out a silver revolver which glinted in the night like gems on black velvet. My brother retreated and I thought I was going to piss my pants, but Pop didn't budge an inch. "Fuck you and your family!" Ray leveled the gun at my father.

Before I could blink, Pop snatched the gun from Ray's hand. Ray was utterly stunned and was about to say something when—*fuacata, fuacata*—my father slapped him twice across the face and the impact sent Ray's hat flying. Pop aimed the gun between his terrified brown eyes.

"*Nunca* . . . never insult my family."

I watched in disbelief as a dark stain formed along Ray's sharkskin pant leg and a puddle of urine spread out around his black suede playboy shoes.

"You think this makes you so tough?" My father cocked the hammer of the gun and Ray began to tremble in fear. "You call yourself a man? The way you treat your woman like she was trash from the street? You slap her around and call her a whore. Out here in the middle of the night disturbing hardworking people and their children. *Tu no eres hombre*. You are nothing. *Eres mierda*. You're worth less than dog shit on the bottom of my shoe," Pop said, then spat in Ray's face. But Ray didn't move, didn't even dare breathe. "You have no respect, no honor. You are a two-bit punk and it shames me that you are Puerto Rican."

Tears began to run down Ray's pockmarked face, his expression a combination of shock and shame. His shoulders slumped, his body heaved, and he began to sob. So grown men did cry after all.

"Please forgive me, Don Paco. I don't mean to be like this, it's the . . . I . . . I drink sometimes . . . and I can't control myself."

Still looking up at the much taller man, my father shook his head in disgust and slowly waved his index finger.

"I don't want to hear any excuses—*si eres hombre, portate como hombre*. If you're a man, behave like a man." Pop uncocked the hammer of the pistol, flicked the cylinder open, emptied the bullets into the palm of his calloused hand, and flung them to the lot across the street. He dropped the gun in front of Ray and it clattered noisily on the asphalt. In a cryptic tone my father added, "I don't ever want to see your face around here again."

Pop, a proud, compact man, wearing nothing but baggy yellow boxer shorts, turned his back on Ray and walked away without looking back. Flaco stood there for a moment, staring in amazement as the big man continued to weep. Pop entered my room and caught me peering out the window.

"Get to bed. You have school tomorrow."

I dropped the binoculars and immediately hopped into bed, since the last thing I wanted was for him to be mad at me. He soon sat beside me and stroked my cheek, his brown eyes filling with tenderness.

"You okay? Want a glass of milk or something?" I solemnly wagged my head, staring at him in reverence. "You saw what happened?"

My eyes never left his as I replied, "Yes," followed by a feeble nod.

He mussed my hair. "Listen, *m'ijo*, the measure of a man is honor and family. Respect. A gun and a fist do not make you a man." He pointed to his temple and said, "This here," then he pointed to his heart and added, "and here are what make you a man. *Entiendes?*"

"*Sí*, Papi."

"Good. Now get some sleep," he said, planting a big kiss on my forehead. I wrapped my arms around his neck and he held me tight. I never felt safer. "I love you, Daniel."

"I love you too, Pop."

He kissed me again and went off to the kitchen to make himself a midnight snack.

Flaco finally returned, grinned, and dove into his bed, which creaked and whined from the impact. *"El viejo*—the old man is wild," he said with a chuckle and shake of the head, then went right back to sleep as if nothing had happened.

I tried to fall asleep but couldn't. Completely wired from the events I'd witnessed, I gazed thoughtfully at the superhero posters and drawings prominently displayed on the wall. Right then and there I decided I was going create a new character, a Puerto Rican superhero named Marine Tiger—strong, fearless, and honorable. Just like my pops.

Walk amidst the Broken Beds

by Staceyann Chin

Walk amidst the broken beds
languishing careless atop cans of rusted food

it is almost impossible to see
there is still life
here

still poetry
between the legs

of chairs
torn skirts
deserted lives exposed vulgar to the tongue of a wind
licking greedy at the flesh of thighs

squatting regretful over public toilets
public assistance
public schools closed in on themselves
like flowers pruning without sun

without children

the authorities say
classrooms must remain
locked
until there are bodies enough to fill them

those displaced
refuse to return their children to rooms
unless there are enough open doors
for them to walk through

the cycle ties us
black and anchored to a History of silence and song

New Orleans lies naked
brutal
a visible example to all who denied
race is roped vicious to opportunity
and tragedy
in America

in this country
in the world
Lakeview is only metaphor for Compton
for Red Hook
for Trenchtown
for Redfern
for the entire motherfucking continent of Africa

only in this instant
the nation gawks at the details of the tragedy
so we can pretend we care about the despair that litters the sidewalks
the porches
the places that used to be lawns

now that the shit has hit the proverbial fan
the properties of the poor can be cut up
and sold to those with the funds to fly south for the bidding

one year
the authorities decreed
one year

and the deeds become fair game
to those for whom Katrina
is an abstract memory of something that happened
to someone else's roof

and just like magic
or racism

an entire city is restructured
for the pleasure of pickpockets and pundits
pontificating on why who should have left
before the levees broke

hard as this may be to hear: the levees in New Orleans broke
because black people across America
don't vote enough
for any presidential administration to care what we think or feel
or what the fuck we may or may not survive

I miss the New Orleans of blue skies and yellow houses
and arms wide open
hips breaking easy over plates of fried catfish
cooked by women who believed
if they couldn't pay you for poetry
they could at least fatten you up for the next city

it was the year 2000 and I ate poems seasoned
by the hands of black women painting prisms
of candor and color

those poems are still here
I hear them humming pungent beneath the bones buried without ceremony
under the rubble
whole pages of rage and reparation remain ripe
for those who wish to scream them

stories disguised as horns
disguised as protest
disguised as grief

poems
grinning guileless from the gums of babies
born after that awful summer
poems inspiring
new teeth
old tongues
hybrid tales told through the rebel ghosts rising dangerous
from the breath of the dead who are begging for us to write them

Broke-Down Princess

by kelly a. abel

*I am so sick of Mommy! This is the third time she promised that we would go see
Daddy and now she changin' her mind again. She don't understand how much
I need to see my daddy. I don't care what he done to her. He still my daddy and I
need to SEE HIM!!*

Shawntaya screamed into her pillow. She knew that if her mother heard
her, she would get another swift crack across the back of the head for acting foolish again. Foolish. That's all Gina ever called Shawntaya. Gina had
little tolerance for Shawntaya's emotional antics. She was a stern woman
with anger branded on her face. Gina's eyebrows were permanently knitted. The only sparkle that remained in her almond-shaped, light brown
eyes was that of a tempered glass surface. She was very difficult to read and
anyone who tried would be quickly put in his place by means of a violent
tongue lashing.

Shawntaya's silent, tearful tantrum spun her mercilessly through emotional exhaustion into a deep, dark sleep. Meanwhile, Gina sat in the
kitchen, staring at a grease spot on the wall. She sat there, fixated on its
shape, trying not to let her emotions get the best of her. For some reason,
out of all the arguments between them, this one actually made her eyes
moisten. She had fought back tears while she reprimanded her daughter
today and she couldn't understand why. The argument had subsided over
an hour ago, and here she sat, emotionally drained, still trying not to think
about the dilemma at hand, still trying to force emotion away from her tear
ducts.

*What the hell am I going to do? This nigga is in jail! I can't be bringin' my
daughter to no jail cell to see this mothafucka! What she knows about her father
are the good times, when we was a happy family and lived over on Asch Loop. What
she knows is playin' with her father and going to Rye Playland and the park and
all that. She don't need to know nothin' about him and them silly niggas from the*

Polo Grounds and the drugs and . . . Oh, God. I miss my husband so much, but he almost had us killed. I'm just tryin' to protect what's left of this family and I cannot explain this to her. What the hell! I shouldn't have to. She needs to listen to me and that's that.

Gina walked to the freezer and pulled out her personal stash, a pint of Häagen-Dazs strawberry ice cream. She cut herself a piece of pound cake and mashed it inside of the ice cream container. It was getting late and she hadn't even started the research paper for her Child Psychology class. It crossed her mind to get into gear and start writing an outline, but she shelved that idea. Instead, she parked her behind on the sofa and let refined sugar and Lifetime take her away from it all.

Gina noticed her ass getting wider. She used to take pride in her appearance. Gina reminisced about her heyday in the eighties. She remembered riding in Audis with the flyest hustlers around the way. She thought about the numerous shopping sprees and the joy she felt when she counted her many fur coats and tailor-made velvet warm-up suits. Her shoes were always dyed to match her clothes to a tee. Her mushroom hairdo was always shiny and fresh. She remembered going to the car shows in Harlem. Gina never owned a car, but she was always that fly, light-skinned honey dip with the pretty eyes on the passenger side. Petite. Sexy. The baddest bitch on the block.

There she sat, lost in her youthful memories. They seemed so long ago. She began to question if any of those great times ever actually happened. She was forty and she was alone. She was a single mother. She was struggling with the rent, the bills, and everything else that came her way with a dollar amount. She looked around her modest apartment. No, it wasn't a penthouse on Park Avenue, but it was hers. Man or no man.

Damn you, Spade.

The amber light of the late-summer sunset began to draw away from the walls of their two-bedroom co-op. The warmth receded into a cool darkness on the white walls. Night had fallen and the house was quiet once again.

Shawntaya woke up around ten o'clock. Her face felt weird and hot. Her sinuses felt strangely dry. She hoped she was getting sick.

People are always nice to you when you get sick.

Suddenly, her ringing cell phone broke the silence. She reached over her nightstand to pick it up, knocking over a can of Sunkist on the way. She cursed under her breath and looked at the phone. It was Maurice, her most favorite boy (excluding Bow Wow) in the whole world.

"Hey, whassup?" She tried to play it cool but her voice always registered about four octaves higher than normal when she spoke to a boy, especially this boy.

"Hey, Taya! What's good?" Maurice had a smile in his voice.

"Chillin'," she giggled. Shawntaya was only thirteen. Chuckling and blushing had become her trademark.

"Yo, why don't you come through and holla at ya boy?"

Maurice was twenty-two. More importantly, Maurice was also referred to as Pimp Baby. This nickname wasn't given to him because of his notoriety for fucking underage girls. No, Maurice, less than an inch shy of six feet, was Pimp Baby because of his baby-face features, smooth and unscathed. His close-cropped hair was lined with precision. His look was deceptive. He appeared younger than his age and mainly attracted junior high girls. Approaching women his own age turned Maurice off. He found girls in their twenties to be too opinionated and demanding. Young girls, on the other hand, knew how to listen.

"I don't know, it's late and my mom is home. We had a fight today and I don't think . . ."

"That's your problem, Taya, you thinkin' too much. Don't you love me?"

Her eyes grew with delightful surprise. He had never used that word before. He hadn't even used that word when he taught her how to suck his dick. He said he was going to show her how to treat a man right. He said that if she could be good at this, no man would ever leave her because every man likes it when a woman can give good head. Shawntaya took those words to heart and obeyed him. She wanted to please him. She was an eager student and Maurice was more than willing to teach.

"Taya, you there?" His voice grew stern.

"Yes, I love you."

"Aiight! So come on through." He was smiling again.

"Okay. Maurice?"

"What up?"

"You love me?" She pressed the phone tightly to her ear in anticipation.

"What? Oh yeah, girl! You know I care about you. Now come on, Daddy's waiting!"

"Okay, I'll be there in a few."

Maurice hung up the phone before she got a chance to say goodbye. Shawntaya didn't notice. She was in love! Her head swam in hysterical elation as she tried to put together a sexy outfit to please her man. She had a man! She searched her closet for clothes that showed what a mature woman she had become. Everything looked so babyish though. She had a lot of designer clothes. One thing her mother was good for was finding deals on designer gear. Everything still looked young. She opted to wear a Baby Phat baby-T and her new Apple Bottoms. She went into her mother's room and ransacked the underwear drawer for a sexy thong. She found one, hot pink with rhinestones.

Oooh, Mommy, you freak.

She ran back to her room and stood in front of the full-length mirror in the nude. She put on the thong and stood there staring at her premature figure. Shawntaya was still shrouded in baby fat. She was developing breasts, but because of her junior-plus-size stature, one would wonder if she'd have any breasts left if she lost weight. Her body was shapeless. It was a mass of plump, tender fat that bounced within its own tawny buoyancy. She was satisfied with her figure because the boys in her class referred to her as *thick* and often made comments on how they wanted to suck on her fat titties. She would return the compliments with angry, sharp glances, learned from her mother, and turn away, giggling hysterically with her chubby fingers over her sheer gloss-stained lips. She stood there in her mother's thong caressing where the future curves of her body would take form.

Yeah, I look real sexy.

Shawntaya put on her outfit. She pulled up the straps of her mother's thong so that they would be revealed above her jeans.

That's the way Beyoncé and them do it.

She applied her makeup, which only consisted of a thick application of cherry lip gloss. Shawntaya brushed out her doobie and let her thick, jet-black hair bounce softly around her shoulders. She looked in the mirror one more time. Her physique was a mass of hills and valleys. Her jeans were too tight and pushed the bulge from her belly over a button that was ready to explode from her waistband. The baby-T was too small. It revealed her plump young stomach and the cavernous hole that was her navel. She wore no bra. Her ripe titties were spread widely apart and sat half-sagging, half-perky on her chest. The thong accentuated her fat by tearing into her flesh. The straps of her thong were barely visible, hiding deep in her folds. All that was visible was an oddly shaped mound of young meat around her waist with an occasional flash of hot pink.

I look good.

Shawntaya grabbed her cell phone and backpack. She stopped in her mother's bedroom and stole twenty dollars from her purse in the closet. She crept silently through the hallway and saw the blue haze from the television brightening an otherwise darkened living room. Shawntaya peeked around the wall and saw her mother sleeping on the sofa. She had been eating ice cream.

Fat bitch. Talkin' about how I need to lose weight. Look at her.

Shawntaya mustered up all of her courage and walked to the front door. She turned the locks slowly, trying not to make the hard and heavy clicking sound of many Co-op City apartment doors. She looked back at her mother one more time. Gina did not stir. Shawntaya closed the door behind her softly and locked it with several light clicks. She had snuck out before. She was becoming a professional.

Gina had a lot on her plate. Between her career as a caseworker for Child Protection Services and finishing her master's degree in Social Work, she didn't have much time for herself. One facet of her life that brought her solace was her daughter's age. Shawntaya wasn't a little girl anymore. Her daughter was able to cook, clean, and mind herself. It took a lot of pressure off, not having to find child care.

She couldn't remember the last time she went on a date. Loneliness began to set in more deeply than it had since Spade got locked up. Spade had been her childhood sweetheart. They reconnected fourteen years ago and fell in love, all over again, immediately. Gina had never felt so complete in her entire life. He was her rock and she was his little mama. It seemed ideal. Although Spade was still in the game and his future was never certain, she married him. She also married him because she was pregnant with Shawntaya. Gina was used to being a hustler's wife. She had been dating drug dealers and boosters all her life. However, Spade was the first and only one she ever loved this intensely. Gina looked out the window of the bus. The Bx30 made its turn around Bartow Avenue and she would be home shortly. The loneliness consumed her. Spade wasn't coming home anytime soon. With two prior felonies and the violation on his parole, Spade was sentenced twenty-five years to life for drug trafficking and conspiracy. She remembered how her heart fell from her chest to her stomach when she heard the verdict. She thought she was going to die. As she watched the court officers take her man away, she felt her insides grow cold. It was like someone had blown out the fire that made her smile. That was six years ago.

The bus rounded the corner onto Co-op City Boulevard. For some reason, Gina thought about her father passing away. He died over fifteen years ago and she had not thought about him for quite some time. Gina loved her daddy, and though her parents were never together, he was always kind and generous to her and her mother. She remembered smelling the Brut aftershave her father wore. The commanding scent always made her think of safety and security. The pride in knowing that she was Daddy's one and only princess had made her feel like she was the only beautiful girl on the planet.

She was so consumed by her thoughts that she almost missed her stop. She stumbled out the back door of the bus and fell onto the concrete below with full impact. The bus pulled away, leaving a black trail of exhaust circling around her head. She lay on the ground and covered her face. Her knees hurt and she was embarrassed.

Then something inside of her broke. She cried. She cried uncontrollably. So many tears flowed that she couldn't feel the surface of her skin when she tried to wipe them away. So she gave in to it. She lay right there, on that sidewalk, in pain that traveled from the depths of her soul to the fresh wounds on her knees. She cried until she felt herself grow light. She cried until she felt herself float away. She cried until she was able to laugh. She stood up and laughed and cried herself all the way down Carver Loop. She laughed a little less when she got to the mailbox in the lobby and collected her bills. She laughed a little more when she read the sign on the elevator door warning tenants to stop stealing shopping carts from the Stop & Shop across the street. She stepped into the elevator and pressed the button for the eighteenth floor.

Things are not so bad. I struggled for years to get to this point. I have a degree and I have all of my teeth, so fuck it. I need to talk to Shawntaya. We got to work through this. She must be hurting and I think I can understand a little more. Things will get better. I can't believe we still hot with each other over seeing her father. It's been almost a month since we had that fight. I gotta make things right for my baby. I gotta make things right for us . . .

Gina stepped off the elevator and walked toward the apartment door. To her surprise it was open. She reached into her shoulder bag and pulled out her .22 caliber pistol. Several experiences at various client home visits had compelled her to protect herself effectively. She walked in quietly. She closed the door softly, leaving it slightly ajar so as not to let it make that clicking sound. Her heart was pounding in her throat and she forgot about the pain pulsating from her scraped-up knees. As she tried to focus and push the sounds of fear from her mind, she began to hear something.

Moaning. Her baby.

Gina crept to her daughter's bedroom. The door was wide open. She would never have been able to prepare herself for what she was about to see.

There was her baby, butt naked on all fours, having sex with two grown men. One, dark-skinned and muscular, was pumping his filthy dick deep inside of her child's young, ripe bottom. His dry, roughened hands had a firm, aggressive grip on her buttocks as she thrust her ass into his densely nappy crotch. The man had his head thrown back and his eyes shut tightly.

"Ahh, this little pussy is so tight. Ahh, shit, you could fuck, little girl. Ahhh . . ." he moaned under his breath. He sounded Jamaican or something.

There was another grown man, a little bit older. He looked a lot like Gerald Levert, stocky with a large belly. Nappy hair sprinkled his entire chest, stomach, and back. Little Shawntaya was sucking this man's dick. She was moaning and moving her head rhythmically around his shaft. This man made no sound. He knelt before her child, grabbing her hair, pumping his groin into her face. He breathed heavily through his gaping mouth while staring down at Shawntaya's plump baby face.

Gina was paralyzed with shock. Suddenly the bathroom door flew open. A younger man came out, zipping up his fly and looking at Gina like she was the intruder.

"Who you?" he asked arrogantly.

"WHAT??!!!!" Gina screamed.

All activities ceased abruptly. Shawntaya jumped up from the floor and ran into her closet for cover. She knew what was coming.

Gina remembered the gun in her hand. She pointed it to the ceiling and fired several shots. The weak shriek from each shot was magnified by the bedroom's acoustics. The bullets cut cleanly into the plaster in the ceiling as the smell of burning metal and smoke fell over the room.

"GET THE FUCK OUT OF MY HOUSE BEFORE I SHOOT YOUR DICKS OFF!!!"

The two men in Shawntaya's room tried to calm Gina down as they grabbed their clothes.

"Chill, ma! Ain't no need for all that noise!" one said.

"WHAT!?!?" Gina screeched.

She shot the one man in the hand.

"GET OUT OF MY HOUSE NOW OR I WILL KILL YOU!!!"

All three men ran from the apartment, barely dressed. The door slammed aggressively, sounding a deep hollow echo down the corridor.

Gina took one step forward toward her daughter's bedroom. She stopped at the doorway. She couldn't bring herself to go inside. She looked around. The soft, pink plush carpet was littered with evidence of debauchery. A half-empty bottle of Christian Brothers was knocked over, leaving a stagnant puddle. She saw one pair of men's jockey shorts, three socks, and two belts scattered randomly around the room. She looked at the closet and saw her daughter's naked buttocks exposed through the open space of the door. Gina stepped back from the doorway. She covered her face with both hands. She was shocked by what she had witnessed and terrified by what she did not see.

Not one condom. Not one condom wrapper.

Jesus Christ . . . my child.

"Shawn," she said quietly. "Clean up this mess." Gina walked away and sat in her kitchen. She left her daughter's door wide open.

Shawntaya was scared to death. She was exposed. Everything she had been doing and everything she had been hiding over the past few months was out in the open. There was no way to cover it up. There was no lie she could tell to put her mother's suspicions at ease. Her face grew warm. Even her tears felt hot as she wiped them away with the back of her reddened hand. Gina had never reacted to her like this before. Then again, her mother had never seen her having sex before. Shawntaya didn't know what to expect. As she crawled out from inside of the closet, she began to pray for the deliverance of her soul because she was positive that this was the last day that she would ever see. She picked up her jeans and T-shirt from off the floor. She sniffed each item, hoping that it didn't reek of weed and cigarettes.

Don't matter much now if Mommy can smell smoke on me. She already gonna kill me.

Shawntaya put on her filthy clothes and started to clean up her room. She hoped that her mother didn't notice the bottle of brandy and the gutted Dutch on her floor. She took her time and picked up each article in hopes of extending the few moments of freedom. The most intimidating prospect was the uncertainty of her mother's plan for discipline. The little girl could not stop crying.

I hope she don't tell Daddy. He would hate me for sure.

Shawntaya heard her mother walking toward her bedroom. Her heart crept into her throat and began to choke her, forcing more tears from her eyes. Her face was on fire, and her stomach sizzled and split in half. She fell to the floor and threw up.

Gina walked past her daughter's bedroom and into the bathroom. She didn't even glance toward her daughter. Shawntaya heard the bathtub running.

What the fuck is she doing? I wish she would just get this over with.

Shawntaya used this opportunity to run to the kitchen and grab a few paper towels to clean up the vomit and liquor from her carpet. On her way back to her room, she saw her mother standing in the corridor looking directly at her.

"Take off your clothes and get in the tub, Shawn." Gina stood there with her arms folded. Her expression was unreadable.

Oh my God. She's going to drown me.

"But Mommy, I didn't finish cleaning up." Shawntaya attempted to prolong the time she had left of her life.

"Now, Shawn." Gina was unmoved.

Shawntaya walked to the bathroom and took off her clothes. She stepped into the bath her mother had drawn for her. It was a little hot but it felt good. Her vagina began to burn a little. Dré, Maurice, and Bizzy had put a hurting on her today. They literally ripped her. She had never done anything like that before. Maurice asked her to do it and he was her man. She would have done anything for him. At first she was afraid, but after a few drinks and the L, it got a lot easier. When they started touching her and taking off her clothes, she didn't feel like she was there. Her mind separated from her body. She watched herself doing all of these things she knew she shouldn't have been doing. She couldn't believe that it was happening to her and she reveled in all of the attention she received from the men. Those men. Dré, Bizzy, and her baby Maurice were the biggest ballers in Co-op. Grown women would want to be in her shoes. At least that's what Shawntaya believed.

Gina's footsteps, steadily tapping the parquet floors, seemed louder than usual. Before she could get up to close the door, Gina walked back into the bathroom. She closed the lid on the toilet seat and sat. She clasped her hands on her lap and looked at the floor.

Shawntaya, ever frightened, began to focus on cleaning her body. She stopped thinking about what had happened with the guys out of fear that her mother could read her mind.

"Who were those men, Shawn?" Gina remained seemingly calm.

"Maurice . . . Dré, Bizzy," Shawntaya whispered.

"Maurice was that boy that came from the bathroom. Anna's son from Section Four. I thought I recognized him. He's in his twenties . . . isn't he?" Gina felt her rage flaring. She was very angry but she wasn't sure where to place it.

"Yeah," Shawntaya whispered. "He's my boyfriend." She figured she might as well start telling the truth if she was going to die anyway.

"He's your *what*?" Gina's voice rose a decibel. "He's a grown man."

"He say he love me."

Gina looked at her daughter and paused briefly. She took a deep breath.

"Who were those other men?" Her voice softened.

"I don't know. His boys."

"Shawn, if he loved you . . . really loved you . . . do you think that he would let other men have sex with you?"

"I don't know."

The tub faucet dripped in a slow, light rhythm. The fluorescent light-bulbs over the vanity mirror released a steady melancholy hum. The syncopated breathing between mother and daughter created a barely audible harmony. Together they created music within silence. No words were spoken. Yet with every breath they were starting to find peace with each other within the complexity of the moment.

"Mommy, I'm bleeding," Shawntaya finally said.

Gina rose from the toilet seat and knelt next to the tub. Her eyebrows knitted upwards with concern.

"Did they hurt you? Did they do something to you inside?"

"No," Shawntaya said with shame. "I think I finally got my period."

"Oh." Gina wasn't sure if she could process any more information about her daughter. "Well, you are about that age. When you get out of the tub, I'll give you some pads . . . I'll show you how to take care if it."

"Okay." Shawntaya looked at her mother and began to cry. "Mommy, I don't know why I did it. I'm sorry. I'm scared. I don't know what I'm doing. Don't tell Daddy, please."

"It's okay, baby. What you did wasn't okay. You messed up, but it's over. You made a mistake. I messed up too. I should have been there to talk to you . . ."

Shawntaya stepped out of the tub. Gina looked at her daughter's blossoming body. She tried to erase the images of those men defiling her child. She grabbed a towel and wrapped it around her daughter. Gina held Shawntaya close to her and kissed the top of her head.

"Baby, I love you and everything is going to be fine, but I still have to ground you . . . You know this, don't you?"

"Yeah."

"Hmm, you know what I think we should do?"

"Nuh-uh." Shawntaya felt waves of relief rippling through her soul. She was going to live.

"Let's write a letter to Daddy."

"You gonna tell him?" Shawntaya felt fear creeping over her again.

"No, no. Just a little something to say hello . . ."

A Debt to Pay

by Carol Taylor

At four a.m. the deserted city street was black and uninviting. Don swallowed hard hoping to moisten his parched throat. It didn't work. When a cat overturned a garbage can lid the deafening clatter made him jump and shriek like a bitch.

He looked around quickly. What was he doing here? He shoulda been outta New York. Hell, he shoulda been on a whole goddamn different coast by now. Hanging round the city with a contract on your head accepted by Black was suicide. Don gave a deranged chuckle. Suicide shit—more like murder, if Black caught up with you. But what did it matter? If the stories were true, Black would haunt him across a dozen cities and states. The only way out was either Black killed you or you killed Black. Don was betting his life on the latter as he got a firmer grip on the revolver in his pocket. He pushed the Kangol up on his forehead and wiped his wet brow with the back of a cuff, leaving a grimy streak on the lily-white fabric. He may have been a murdering pimp, but Dapper Diamond Don was always well turned out.

A devilishly handsome man, Diamond Don also had the gift of words. Back in the day, girls weren't above murder to get into his stable. And he'd never been above murder for any reason. He chuckled evilly: This one ho he'd had to beat down almost dead to keep her black ass acquiescent. Hell, back in the day, he'd been the biggest mack daddy pimp uptown. Bitches was standing in line to suck his dick. And he had plenty dick to go round. Diamond chuckled again. Ah, those was the days. But now, times they were a-changin'. Fewer girls on the stroll. The ones walkin' wanna work for theyselves. Could you imagine, whores pimpin' theyselves? Don shook his head. This feminist shit was gettin' way outta hand.

But that was the least of his problems right now. He had Black on his ass, 'bout close to a week now. It had to be Black. Diamond could almost smell him. And everybody avoiding him like the fucking plague. And when Black took your contract it was the muthafucking Black Plague 'cause somebody was gonna end up dead fo' sho'. Yeah, the writing was on the wall. His number had come up. But Black had better be man enough to take him. Diamond didn't become one of the top pimps in Harlem to go out like some bitch. And for some dead ho. Shit, plenty dead hoes in his past. But this one had to be kin to Black. He laughed; even murdering muthafuckas got family too. Just Don's dumb luck.

The bitch had been asking for it though. Sniffing round him all the time. Wanting this, wanting that. Pushin' them titties up in his face and shakin' that fat ass. She hadn't thought she was racking up a debt? And with them commercial curves, she'd be a guaranteed moneymaker on the stroll. Don was gonna make a mint off her. Just had to break her in first. And look what she went and done. 'Cause of a little dick? He ain't even put it on her hard. But she had to go swallow a sleeping pill cocktail with a malt liquor chaser.

A virgin. Shit. And sixteen. She'd said she was eighteen. Hell, she'd looked at least twenty. They sho' was growin' 'em big these days. Don sighed. She's the one went and fucked up. She was green, man. Fucked-up shit happen every muthafucking day and the dumb bitch had to go kill herself over it. Who knew she had family? Mother, father, sister. They shoulda kept a better tab on her. Now she dead, they gon' put a hit on him. And goddamn Black was try'na collect. Ain't that a mutha?

He didn't know much about this Black cat, just gossip, whispers about people disappearing. Some kinda silent, shadowy figure. A hat pulled low, big lips, a slight frame, black leather gloves and boots. And always cloaked in the deepest, darkest midnight. So dark you didn't see him until you was almost dead. Hah, that was a nursery tale to frighten young boys into staying square. It was far too late for Diamond; either way, he knew the stories couldn't be true. Black was just another hustler, same as him. 'Cept Black traded in death, not flesh. Stone-cold killer. Didn't care about the mark, just the job.

Diamond stopped in front of the Apollo and looked down the empty avenue for a gypsy cab. He wanted off the street. Something didn't feel right. Not one car in sight. Damn. He'd have to hop the 4 uptown to the Bronx. He longed for his El Dorado, but he'd lost his choice ride doing a bid. This Dominican cat who owned a domino spot took it as payment for an old debt. That was the thing about debt: You always paid it, one way or another.

Unknown to Diamond Don, Black was standing about five feet to his right in a darkened doorway. Not a man known for subtlety, Diamond had been easy to find. Black had learned early in the game: To catch a rat, find the people who most want him trapped. With Diamond Don that meant just about everybody. Not much street love for an over-the-hill pimp, the north side of thirty-five, who was fast losing the bling and bucks to ensnare a fresh stable of young whores. The few of his girls left were ready to jump and his boys all wanted him dead. It was understandable; Diamond was an evil man, who, drunk on perceived power, had thrown out the rules of the street for his own type of twisted law. The rape of a sixteen-year-old square had secured his place in Hell with a quickness. And Black was looking forward to seeing him off.

Black flicked flame to a cigarette and exhaled a gray poltergeist of smoke. Diamond inhaled sharply. He hadn't known someone was there. A slight figure, cloaked in black, with a hat pulled low across her face.

Black smiled, cocked the hammer, and looking Don in the eyes, pulled off her hat. Her face was almost identical to her dead sister's. Then she pulled the trigger and blew him to Hell.

Love Letter to Haiti

by Natasha Labaze

Haiti was my first love and, like any love, I don't remember when I fell in love with her. I just hear the story of a love-torn five-year-old girl crying and refusing to leave her, a distraught and confused little girl returning to the United States, her birth land, with the nostalgia of cassava and mamba and *pâte corde*. "Haiti, leave it or love it" has turned into, "Haiti, leave it and love it." To love her, you'd have to leave her. "*Ayiti cheri, pi bel peyi pase ou nan pwen, fo mwen te kite ou, poum te kon vale.*" ("Beloved Haiti, there is no country as beautiful. I had to leave you to know your worth.") So many of us have had to leave, to brush our lovesteps unto other shores.

Haiti. She is beautiful and neglected. (Should I say beautifully neglected?) She carries within her womb-scented flowers blooming fruit trees, dust-powdered, eroded mountains, and, above all, hungry children. When I descend upon her wound, feel the hot sun hit my forehead, hear the sound of the drums played for the tourists—tourists who are actually Haiti's lost children born abroad—and wait on line for my suitcases, the pungent smell of sweat from working women and men drifts toward me. I inhale this stench of labor and poverty with passion.

How dare I romanticize poverty. Once my suitcases have been dragged and investigated, searched for drugs that come and leave this country like coffee grinds running through a torn-cloth filter, I relish the hostile voices. Men and boys fight to get the job to carry my bags to the car. Then behind the gates, I see the faces of some who will never get to see *lot bo* (the other side). The gate itself is a barrier distinguishing the haves from the have-nots, those who have visas from those who don't, those who were born in Haiti from those who were born *lot bo*.

As I pass the threshold, I subconsciously embrace the fluidity that my North American birthright has given me, and the sociopolitical consciousness of my Haitian heritage. (Writing this piece, I realize how condescending I sound . . .) I join in the cadence of the Haitian lifestyle. I tip the quarrelling luggage helpers with American dollars that I saved so as not to get insulted. I'm told by my mother to tip only one helper, but I tip everyone who surrounds me. After this initial battle, I settle down in the back of the car, screen out the petty conversation—about the weather, about relatives who no longer come to Haiti—and I finally take a look at my beloved, whom I've left for a year or two. The merchant women and men still walk down the dusty road with torn sandals as the sun settles behind the mountains one more time. The colorful houses in need of paint still stand crooked and proud.

It's as if I never left. Haiti, why can't I stop loving you? You've been the bane and essence of my existence. Your dark cool night air still calls me. When I am hungry, I think, *How can a child wake up and sleep in hunger?* I wish I could feed all the children of Haiti, empower them with confidence and a thirst for knowledge, establish solid public libraries in the city and rural areas. Oh Haiti, how I love thee, let me count the ways. I love it when your burning sun tarnishes me; I love it when you quench my thirst with freshly squeezed, naturally sweet orange juice like I have never tasted before. Haiti, Leogane, Kenscoff—your colorful camionettes with the raunchy drivers yelling sexist comments and the loud hip-hop call me. Your dirt-infested streets and the vision (not the reality) of children with empty bellies glaring at half-million-dollar SUVs calls me like the voice of an abusive lover beckoning me sweetly after tearing me apart.

And somehow I still return, not forgetting the pain of the coëxistence of stark discrepancies—bidonvilles sitting side by side with gated mansions—but continuing to savor the swollen wound; pressing down on it as I resist being healed. You slapped me with your sexist comments. You cheated on me with your love for your own, reminding me when I land on your shores that I'm not a true Haitian but a "diaspora." Your neglect has taken away my grandmother, dying while giving life. Your neglect lured my brother into the whirlwind of drugs that you harbor so nonchalantly. Your zephyr carries the scent of inhaled glue, or worse, mixed crack or cocaine from the nostrils of your addicted and lost children.

Oh Haiti, how I love you. I have shunned you for the last five years like a frightened child, wondering how I could be simultaneously loved and abused, wondering how I could love and despise you all at once, how I can flinch from you, yet yearn for you like a scorched soul mesmerized by a mirage of home.

Contributors

KELLY A. ABEL, born and raised in the northeast Bronx, is a photographer currently living in Delaware. This is her first publication.

STACEYANN CHIN is a New Yorker and a Jamaican national, an "out poet and political activist" who credits her achievements to her grandmother's hardworking history and the pain of her mother's absence. A featured performer in the Tony Award–winning *Def Poetry Jam on Broadway*, she is author of the poetry chapbooks *Wildcat Woman* and *Stories Surrounding My Coming*. Chin tries desperately to create room to travel, to see her sister, and to breathe.

BAHIYYIH DAVIS has published work in *South Loop Review*, *Columbia Poetry Review*, and *Hair Trigger*. She is currently working on her B.A. in Fiction Writing and completing a collection of creative nonfiction. She lives in Chicago.

T'AI FREEDOM FORD is a high school English teacher, writer, and performance poet who lives, loves, and survives in the borough of Brooklyn (and sometimes Queens). She has an MFA in Creative Writing/Fiction from Brooklyn College.

MICHAEL A. GONZALES lives in Brooklyn. He has written cover stories for *Essence*, *Latina*, *Vibe*, and *XXL*. His essay on pimp culture, "Cashmere Thoughts," appears in the forthcoming *Beats, Rhymes & Life*. This is his second story to appear in BRONX BIANNUAL.

KENJI JASPER'S latest novel is entitled *Snow*. The Brooklyn-based author coëdited the forthcoming *Beats, Rhymes & Life: What We Love and Hate about Hip-hop*, and he curates the urban noir series *The Armory* for Akashic Books.

NATASHA LABAZE is a schoolteacher in Cambridge, Massachusetts. Her parents moved from Haiti to the United States during the 1960s. This is her first publication.

MILES MARSHALL LEWIS lives in Paris, France.

D. SCOT MILLER is a Bay Area poet, visual artist, novelist, and teacher. A founding father of the BlackBard Writing Collective, he is author of *Direction and Car-keys* and *Slicker*. He divides his time between writing, wearing nothing but a bowler hat, and taking care of his son, Tré.

LIZA JESSIE PETERSON is a Philadelphia-born, New York–based actor/poet/playwright. Her plays include the solo shows *Chiron's Homegirl Healer Howls* and *The Peculiar Patriot*. Since 1998, she has facilitated writing workshops with incarcerated adolescents at Rikers Island prison and Bridges Juvenile Center in the Bronx. Her film appearances include *Slam*, *Bamboozled*, and *Love the Hard Way*.

JERRY A. RODRIGUEZ is a theater writer and director whose various plays have been staged off-Broadway at the Actor's Studio, the Nuyorican Poet's Café, and the Village Gate, among others. He directed and produced the 1983 Fearless Four video "Problems of the World (Today)," a landmark in hip-hop music. His first novel, *The Devil's Mambo*, debuts in the spring. Please visit him at www.jerryarodriguez.com.

SÉKOUWRITES is the editor of *When Butterflies Kiss*, a serial novel in which ten authors each wrote one chapter of a single narrative. His most recent fiction has been published in the black erotica anthologies *Wanderlust* and *Caramel Flava*. He holds an MFA in Creative Writing from the New School.

SUN SINGLETON published an essay on the pioneering female rap trio Sequence in *Vibe's Hip-Hop Divas*. Her latest EP as a singer/songwriter is entitled *Believe I*.

CAROL TAYLOR is the editor of the best-selling black erotic fiction series *Brown Sugar* and *Wanderlust: Erotic Travel Tales*. She is working on a novel.

SHEREE RENÉE THOMAS is a Memphian living in New York City. She is editor of the anthologies *Dark Matter: Reading the Bones* and *Dark Matter: A Century of Speculative Fiction from the African Diaspora*, both winners of World Fantasy Awards.

Also from AKASHIC BOOKS

BRONX BIANNUAL, ISSUE NO. 1
edited by Miles Marshall Lewis
184 pages, trade paperback, $14.95

Writing from: Donnell Alexander, Federico Anderson, Dana Crum, Michael A. Gonzales, KRS-One, Michael C. Ladd, Ferentz LaFargue, Reginald Lewis, Adam Mansbach, Caille Millner, muMs, and Greg Tate.

"*Bronx Biannual* does a good job of bringing together a group of interesting authors with a background in hip-hop culture."
—*Urbanology* magazine

"Truly a bi-coastal melting pot of hip-hop culture and ideas . . ."
—*Elemental* magazine

SCARS OF THE SOUL ARE WHY KIDS WEAR BANDAGES WHEN THEY DON'T HAVE BRUISES
by Miles Marshall Lewis
200 pages, trade paperback original, $14.95

"Lewis has composed an observant and urbane B-boy's rites of passage . . . Herein find a hiphop bildungsroman told in prose full of buoyancy and bounce, generously stocked with revelations about black transatlantic culture and romance that are as much a generation's as the writer's own."
—Greg Tate, author of *Flyboy in the Buttermilk*

GOT by D
*Debut title from *The Armory,* a new high-quality urban noir imprint edited by acclaimed novelist Kenji Jasper.
200 pages, trade paperback original, $13.95

"Packed with a rare combination of drama and class, *Got* has all the elements of an urban classic in the vein of *Carlito's Way* and *Bodega Dreams*. Let the poseurs beware: In his first time out, D doesn't just raise the bar on street lit, he broke the damn thing!"
—Black Artemis, author of *Picture Me Rollin'*

TALES OF THE OUT & THE GONE
stories by Amiri Baraka
222 pages, trade paperback original, $14.95

"Baraka is such a provocateur it becomes easy to overlook that he is first and foremost a writer . . . He writes crisp, punchy sentence and has a fine ear for dialogue . . . Reading Baraka's fiction is all about enjoying the journey, and never mind the destination."
—*New York Times Book Review* (Editors' Choice)

BECOMING ABIGAIL by Chris Abani
A selection of the *Essence Magazine* Book Club and Black Expressions Book Club
128 pages, trade paperback original, $11.95

"Compelling and gorgeously written, this is a coming-of-age novella like no other. Chris Abani explores the depths of loss and exploitation with what can only be described as a knowing tenderness. An extraordinary, necessary book."
—Cristina Garcia, author of *Dreaming in Cuban*

A SIMPLE DISTANCE by K.E. Silva
188 pages, trade paperback original, $14.95

"In this soon to be classic novel, K.E. Silva lays the groundwork for redefining family values. Moving back and forth between California and the fictional Caribbean island state of Baobique, Silva paints a picture perfect portrait of a biracial family . . . and masterfully weaves her insights into a delightfully subversive narrative that's anything but simple."
—*Tikkun*

These books are available at local bookstores, or online with a credit card through www.akashicbooks.com. To order by mail, send a check or money order to:

AKASHIC BOOKS
PO Box 1456, New York, NY 10009
www.akashicbooks.com / info@akashicbooks.com

Prices include shipping. Outside the U.S., add $8 to each book ordered.